KURT D. LLOYD ON JURY SELECTION

KURT D. LLOYD ON JURY SELECTION

A TRIAL LAWYER'S MANUAL FOR ILLINOIS

Advantage®

Published by Advantage, Charleston, South Carolina.
Member of Advantage Media Group.

ADVANTAGE is a registered trademark and the Advantage colophon is a trademark of Advantage Media Group, Inc.

Printed in the United States of America.

ISBN: 978-1-59932-812-6
LCCN: 2016956639

Cover design by George Stevens.

To my mother and father who, from humble beginnings, gave me the mind and drive to accomplish many things, including this book.

ABOUT THE AUTHOR

KURT D. LLOYD

Kurt is a plaintiff's trial lawyer who has been engaged in selecting juries for more than thirty years. Before trial, Kurt regularly conducts focus group research for a plaintiff's medical malpractice case to identify potential conscious or hidden juror bias relevant to issues in the case, which must be addressed in jury selection and in framing the winning narrative story. Applying his legal research on jury selection and focus group knowledge and experience, Kurt uses the voir dire questioning process to discover conscious or hidden juror bias and "deselect" those jurors. Kurt's belief is that if the plaintiff's trial lawyer does not overcome juror bias in jury selection, the jury selected will doom the plaintiff's case. Kurt's legal research for this book, combined with his knowledge and skill, has won his clients some of the largest Illinois jury verdicts and settlements against physicians, nurses, and hospitals. He has tried medical malpractice cases in Chicago as well as in many rural towns where jurors often knew each other and the defendant health-care providers. Kurt has won jury verdicts at almost three times the average win rate for medical malpractice cases as a whole. Kurt's jury trials have included delay in diagnosis of cancer, birth injuries, anesthesia mishaps, surgical mistakes, and medication errors.

In 1985, Kurt graduated from IIT Chicago-Kent College of Law. He immediately began as a plaintiff's personal injury lawyer and started practicing jury trial work. In 1990, he obtained his first million-dollar medical malpractice plaintiff's verdict in a rural county where the last thirty-five jury verdicts against physicians had been in favor of the defense. By 1995, Kurt had obtained two record-setting jury verdicts, one against a physician for the wrongful death of a retired widow and another against a managed care physician for brain damage birth injury.

Kurt has held many positions and received many honors and awards as a result of his jury trial accomplishments. From 1995 to 1997, and again in 2007, he was the moderator and planner for medical malpractice seminars for the Illinois Trial Lawyers Association, the most widely attended seminars by fellow Illinois trial lawyers. In 1998, he became an invited member of the prestigious American Board of Trial Advocates, a national organization requiring a minimum of fifty civil jury trials for membership. In 2004, the American Association of Trial Lawyers, now known as the American Association for Justice, awarded Kurt the Citation of Excellence medal for his civil jury trial accomplishments and experience.

In 2007, Kurt lost a major medical malpractice–wrongful death case, which was devastating to him. He later learned from post-verdict juror interviews that some jurors held biases in favor of the defendant physician that prevented a fair trial, which drove Kurt to reinvent his approach to prosecuting the medical malpractice case, including researching, discovering, and overcoming jury bias in favor of the medical profession.

In 2009, Kurt won a record-setting verdict against a neurosurgeon. Again, in 2012, he obtained a record-setting jury verdict against a surgeon in a small rural Illinois county for causing double vision in a retired artist.

During the past five years, Kurt, who has a reputation among Illinois attorneys for finding and presenting leading medical expert witnesses to prosecute the plaintiff's medical malpractice charge, has presented lectures to other trial attorneys on the techniques and strategies for offering winning proof of medical negligence to the jury, including presenting convincing expert witness opinion testimony.

As of September 2016, Kurt has gone to verdict or settled after the jury was selected in more than seventy trials.

Kurt lives in Chicago with his family and continues to try medical malpractice cases for injured patients. Kurt hopes that his efforts protect and promote patient safety.

ABOUT THE BOOK

This manual is designed to be a ready reference for Illinois trial lawyers. The table of contents lists every topic covered, and each topic contains the necessary background and citations. To be concise, male pronouns are generally used rather than "he or she" in generic references to lawyers or jurors even though the author believes Illinois has many fine female lawyers and respects the willingness of women to serve their civic duty as jurors.

TABLE OF CONTENTS

INTRODUCTION

Jury selection is really the process of jury "deselection," or the art of removing prospective jurors who will damage the client's case.

When lawyers show up in court, the jurors who have been brought in, usually thirty-six to forty-two people, have already been selected by pulling names off of jury lists. Collectively, it's a pool of people who presumably are qualified—United States citizens, eighteen or older, and of sound mind and integrity. The art of jury selection is to identify those jurors who carry bias that could affect the client's case. All prospective jurors have inherent bias. Based on past experiences and social relationships, people form a set of beliefs through which they filter everything they see. The lawyer may present compelling facts and evidence to the jury, but unless he knows the inherent biases of the jurors he allowed to be empaneled, he doesn't know how they are going to "see" and interpret those facts. Each juror "sees" facts through his own lens, which has been shaped, shaded, tinted, and polished based on personal experiences, relationships, and beliefs. A juror sees what he believes. He does not believe what he sees.

So jury deselection is the trial lawyer's process of using proper questioning to get prospective jurors to frankly and openly disclose their thoughts about lawyers and lawsuits—including the specific type of case, such as medical malpractice—and find out if they have opinions or beliefs that are going to sink that case and then remove those jurors. I have found that inexperienced lawyers generally don't know the case law well enough to draft acceptable and appropriate questions to find out how a juror feels about giving somebody money for pain and suffering, for example, or suing a doctor. The juror may have a doctor in his family, or he may just think highly of doctors, but until the right question is posed, he really hasn't ever thought of his personal belief that he probably favors doctors over patients. The right questions reveal a juror's past experiences and beliefs so that the lawyer can decide whether that prospective juror is going to look at the case at least in a neutral or fair fashion—and not a biased or negative fashion—toward the client.

Too many times, it is only after juries come back with a defense verdict that a young lawyer for the plaintiff talks to the jurors post-verdict and finds out things he should have known about them. Maybe a juror had somebody in his family who became disabled through nobody's fault and believes, "Well, if they didn't get any money, why should I give you money?" The trial lawyer's failure to expose that kind of biased attitude or negative experience and eliminate that juror can sink a case before the jury hears any evidence or argument.

To be effective at jury deselection, a trial lawyer must understand the laws and rules of voir dire questioning and challenging of objectionable jurors. Many books and articles try to teach the art of voir dire questioning of prospective jurors. Unfortunately, based on this teaching, too many lawyers research and write questions to practice the "art" of voir dire but, once in the courtroom, find out that the case law does not allow the "artful" form of the question they drafted, no matter how clever it is. For example, case law allows questions about a juror's attitudes toward awarding money damages for pain and suffering but does not allow questions about the juror's personal experiences with pain and suffering. Failing to know that distinction, the trial lawyer may not ask the question properly. Incredibly, after multiple objections, the lawyer never discovers the unfavorable, latently biased jurors before it is too late.

More important, too often the trial lawyer is forced to accept unfavorable jurors because his grasp of the law for challenging an objectionable juror is lacking. The trial judge tells the lawyer that his "mere suspicion" that a juror is biased is not good enough to remove the juror, the judge remarks that the suspicious juror has said he can set aside his personal beliefs and be "fair," and he denies the lawyer's request to bounce the juror. Again, the trial lawyer simply does not know the law on the burden of proof required to challenge a juror's personal biases for cause, so that he can effectively question an objectionable juror and get him removed from the jury panel. What person sitting as a potential juror when benignly asked can he be fair will admit to the judge, attorneys, and every other potential juror listening and watching that he is an unfair person? No one. The juror believes—wants to believe—he can be a "good citizen." Secretly, perhaps unconsciously, he does not believe in the trial lawyer's case, does not believe in lawyers and lawsuits, and does not even want to be on the jury because he has no dog in the fight. But he is not going to admit it in public, unless the lawyer knows how to ask the juror a properly allowed question. The trial lawyer must know how to lawfully, properly ask questions to reveal the juror's true beliefs.

This book can be used by any Illinois lawyer who's selecting a jury, whether it's a contract case, a personal injury case, or a criminal or traffic court case. It should be used as a reference while preparing for jury selection and should be sitting on the counsel's table as a manual to argue to the judge in court based on juror answers to questions. The myriad statutes, court rules, and case law for jury selection are listed so that the lawyer can effectively ask appropriate questions, exercise peremptory challenges, and meet the burden of proof necessary to remove an objectionable juror for cause or to rehabilitate and keep a favorable juror. Background is also provided on how to draft motions to provide the broadest possible opportunities for voir dire questions.

Once the trial lawyer learns the intricate laws and rules set forth in this manual, many questions can be properly designed and asked to discover the rogue juror quietly waiting to be chosen. A trial lawyer may spend years preparing a case on behalf of a client. When the client's day in court finally comes, everyone has a lot at stake. This book, and the additional online resources offered in various chapters and in the conclusion, aims to make sure that biased jurors don't slip through and interfere with the client getting a fair trial.

CHAPTER 1: HOW ILLINOIS JURIES ARE SELECTED

The trial lawyer does not select any of the citizens summoned to court as prospective jurors. The Illinois legislature has enacted a statutory scheme by which citizens are selected as eligible jurors from jury lists and summoned to court.

The Illinois Jury Act provides for summoning prospective jurors who are adult US citizens:

> free from all legal exception, of fair character, of approved integrity, of sound judgment, well informed, and able to understand the English language, whether in spoken or written form or interpreted into sign language. 705 ILCS 305/2 (1998).

To assure the right to an impartial jury, the Illinois legislature has granted both the plaintiff and the defendant peremptory rights to remove a number of prospective, qualified jurors for any reason—for example, mere suspicion of bias. 735 ILCS 5/2-1106(a). The legislature has also granted the right to challenge for cause and remove any juror based on evidence of impartiality. 735 ILCS 5/2-1101 (1984). How the trial lawyer effectively exercises these alternative rights of deselection is explored in depth in chapters 5 and 6. This chapter covers the statutory qualifications.

1.1. SUMMONING THE POTENTIAL JURORS TO COURT

In Illinois, prospective jurors are summoned to court using a statutory scheme for creating a jury list of qualified jurors. The clerk's office brings a number of those jurors to a specific courtroom, where the trial judge randomly puts twelve jurors in the box. From that point, the experience of the trial lawyers in conducting jury selection helps determine how many of the summoned citizens are questioned or dismissed without questioning because they are not needed for any cases currently going to trial.

1.1.a. Jury List of Potential Jurors

Under the Illinois Jury Act, a jury list is created each year by each county pursuant to 705 ILCS 305/1 consisting of the following persons of the county:

- legal voters;
- Illinois driver's license holders;
- Illinois Identification Card holders;
- Illinois Person with a Disability Identification Card holders; and
- claimants for unemployment insurance.

1.1.b. Statutory Juror Qualifications (705 ILCS 305/2)

In all counties in Illinois, jurors must have the legal qualifications prescribed by statute. The juror qualification statute, 705 ILCS 305/2, provides that prospective jurors must be:

- inhabitants of the county;
- of the age of eighteen years or upward;
- free from all legal exception, of fair character, of approved integrity, of sound judgment, well informed, and able to understand the English language, whether in spoken or written form or interpreted into sign language; and
- citizens of the United States of America.

The statute does not define the terms "legal exception, of fair character, of approved integrity, of sound judgment, [and] well informed . . ." Presumably, the voir dire process confirms these character traits.

1.1.c. **Statutory Juror Disqualification (705 ILCS 305/14)**

In Illinois, a prospective juror who has been summoned may become statutorily disqualified to serve on a jury. The juror disqualification statute, 705 ILCS 305/14, provides:

> It shall be sufficient cause of challenge of a petit juror that
>
> - he lacks any one of the qualifications mentioned in Section 2 of this Act; or
> - if he is not one of the regular panel, that he has served as a juror on the trial of a cause in any court in the county within one year previous to the time of his being offered as a juror; or
> - he is a party to a suit pending for trial in that court.
> - It shall be the duty of the court to discharge from the panel all jurors who do not possess the qualifications provided in this Act, as soon as the fact is discovered.
> - If a person has served on a jury in a court within one year, he shall be exempt from again serving during such year, unless he waives such exemption.

1.1.c.1. **Juror Hardship (705 ILCS 305/10.02)**

The hardship statute, 705 ILCS 305/10.02, provides in pertinent part:

Under paragraph (a), a prospective juror shall be excused who "shows that such service would impose an undue hardship on account of the nature of the prospective juror's occupation, business affairs, physical health, family situation, active duty in the National Guard or Illinois Naval Militia or other personal affairs…"

Under paragraph (b), a "family situation" is defined as a "… prospective juror being the primary care giver of a person with a mental or physical disability, a person with a medically diagnosed behavior disorder."

This hardship statute permits a county jury administrator to excuse jurors for hardship. In Illinois, there are not any reported cases regarding a trial judge's discretion to find a prospective juror would suffer an undue hardship if he were to serve on a jury. Further, the statute does not define "mental or physical disability." However, a trial judge has broad discretion to find that a prospective juror would not be able to serve effectively.

1.1.c.2. **Nursing Mothers**

Under 705 ILCS 305/10.3 (2006), any mother nursing her child shall, upon request, be excused from jury service.

1.1.c.3. **Juror's Total and Permanent Disability**

Under 705 ILCS 305/10.4 (2016), a juror who has "total and permanent disability" is excused from jury service. The term "total and permanent disability" means any physical or mental impairment, disease, or loss of a permanent nature that prevents performance of the duties of a juror. It does not mean an "impairment or disease" that is transitory or minor in nature and capable of being improved.

1.1.d. **Excusing Prospective Jurors for Statutory Disqualification**

Under 705 ILCS 305/14, a prospective juror who is statutorily disqualified must be excused by the court for cause. If the trial judge is aware of any fact or evidence that a prospective jury is statutorily unqualified to serve, the trial judge has a duty to excuse the juror. *People v. O'Malley*, 143 Ill. App.3d 474 (1st D. 1986). The trial judge has no discretion to allow the juror to sit if he is statutorily disqualified. *Id.* However, if the trial judge refuses to excuse a juror who is statutorily disqualified, the party objecting must use or exhaust any remaining peremptory challenges available to preserve the issue for appeal. *People v. Ford*, 19 Ill. 2d 466 (1960); *People v. Cunningham*, 123 Ill. App.2d 190 (1st D. 1970).

Under 705 ILCS 305/14, a prospective juror who lacks any of the basic qualifications under 705 ILCS 305/2 must be excused, including lack of the following prerequisites:

- US citizenship
- legal age of eighteen
- inhabitant of the county
- able to understand the English language in written and spoken form (including through sign language, if necessary)

Under 705 ILCS 305/14, a prospective juror is also disqualified for the following reasons:

- juror has served as a juror in any court in the [same] county within the previous year;
- juror is a party to a suit pending for trial in that court.

A juror who is a party to a lawsuit pending for trial must be removed, despite testifying under oath that he can remain fair and impartial. *People v. O'Malley*, 143 Ill. App.3d 474, 478, 493 N.E.2d 82, 84 (1st D. 1986). No further showing of prejudice is required. The trial judge does not have discretion under the statute and must remove the juror for cause. *Id.*

Unless the party objecting to the statutorily disqualified jurors exhausts his peremptory challenges and is forced to accept such jurors, his objections to denial for cause will be waived on appeal. *People v. Lake*, 298 Ill. App.3d 50, 55, 697 N.E.2d 1147, 1151 (1st D. 1998). A party must still exhaust his peremptory challenges during jury selection to preserve on appeal the trial judge's error in failing to excuse a statutorily disqualified juror. *People v. Rivera*, 251 Ill. App.3d 375, 621 N.E.2d 179 (1st D. 1993).

1.1.e. **Juror Has a Physical Impairment (735 ILCS 1106)**

The statute on challenging a juror for cause, 735 ILCS 1106, allows removal for physical impairment but does not define what the physical impairment needs to be. So while the Jury Act statute, 705 ILCS 10.04, cited *supra*, involving total and permanent disability, prohibits automatic dismissal for a temporary or partial disability, the trial lawyer can use this statute, which is contained in the Illinois Code of Civil Procedure, to argue that any "physical impairment" makes the prospective juror unable to effectively listen to the evidence and follow the law to render a fair verdict during his service. Because "physical impairment" is not defined, impairment can extend beyond the issue of hearing or understanding the English language under 305 ILCS 305/2. For example, under 735 ILCS 1106, a prospective juror arguably could suffer from a variety of impairments that are not totally disabling, such as narcolepsy, poor eyesight, incontinence, or some impairment that keeps him from sitting for too long. Thus, 735 ILCS 1106 gives the trial judge broad discretion to find that virtually any physical impairment is grounds to remove a prospective juror for cause.

THE PURPOSE OF VOIR DIRE

The purpose of voir dire is to discover those prospective jurors selected as eligible to serve who would be biased against the trial lawyer and his client and remove—i.e., deselect—them. The plaintiffs and the defendants alike have the right to an impartial jury. *Smithers v. Henriquez*, 368 Ill. 588, 598, 15 N.E.2d 499, 504 (1938). In a jury trial, the voir dire process protects the right to an impartial jury by exposing possible biases of potential jurors. *McDonough Power Equipment, Inc. v. Greenwood*, 464 US 548, 554, 104 S.Ct. 845, 849 (1984). The purpose of voir dire examination is the selection of impartial jurors—free from bias and prejudice. *Kingston v. Turner*, 115 Ill. 2d 445, 465 (1987); *People v. Wilson*, 303 Ill. App.3d 1035 (1st D. 1999); *v*, 2 Ill. App.3d 185 (1st D. 1971). The voir dire process is supposed to assure the selection of panels of jurors who are free from bias or prejudice. *Limer v. Casassa*, 273 Ill. App.3d 300 (4th D. 1995).

There are many things a trial lawyer cannot control about jury selection, but he can help ensure that the jurors are statutorily qualified, meaning for example that they are US citizens and they don't have a lawsuit pending in court or a physical disability that disqualifies them. The judge has to remove anyone failing to meet those statutory qualifications. The next chapter will cover how to question jurors to remove them for additional, nonstatutory reasons, also known as challenges for common law cause.

ONLINE RESOURCES

TRIAL LAWYERS SHOULD VISIT THE AUTHOR'S WEBSITE AT KURTDLLOYD.COM AND SUBSCRIBE TO HIS BLOG, LLOYD'S TRIAL NOTEBOOK (LLOYDSTRIALNOTEBOOK.COM), TO DOWNLOAD A COMPENDIUM OF ILLINOIS STATUTES AND COURT RULES APPLICABLE TO JURY SELECTION.

CHAPTER 2: THE VOIR DIRE EXAMINATION PROCESS

All summoned jurors in Illinois are required to complete a short questionnaire, commonly known as a juror card, containing basic information about themselves. A trial lawyer must use this information strategically throughout the jury selection process, beginning with the voir dire examination.

2.1. TWELVE JURORS IN THE BOX

In Illinois, the trial judge is required to call twelve prospective jurors into the jury box for voir dire examination. Although the jurors are chosen in panels of four, the trial lawyer is given copies of all twelve juror cards, with the name, address, marital status, education, and employment background of each juror. The juror card also asks whether they've ever been the victim of a crime, and if so, how many years ago; whether they've ever served on a jury before; and whether they have any hearing impairments.

Knowing the names and basic background of all twelve jurors in the box is important as the trial lawyer decides whether to accept the first panel of four jurors because he knows who is next in order to replace an excused juror. In the following diagram, the blank boxes are filled with strategic information. There, next to the number four, is John Smith, whose juror card says he works for an insurance company. The attorney for a malpractice plaintiff may decide not to remove somebody in the first panel of four because that guy and others in line seem more dangerous than any of the first four. One prospective juror may be dressed like a blue-collar worker and list his employment status as retired, but the juror card gives the prior employment and highest level of education, so an attorney can tell he's a retired hospital executive with a PhD. The juror card provides at least a snapshot of basic information.

PANEL OF FOUR

				4	3
				2	1

A party has a right to have twelve jurors called into the jury box before voir dire commences. 705 ILCS 305/21. See also, *People v. Curran*, 286 Ill. 302, 305 (1918); *Sterling Bridge v. Pearl*, 80 Ill. 251 (1875). Specifically, the Illinois statute provides:

> The court has a duty to call a full number of jurors into the jury box before either party is required to examine the jurors. Either party or the court can insist on this procedure. 705 ILCS 305/21.

The failure to fill the entire jury box is a reversible error. *Chicago City Ry. Co. v. Fetzer*, 113 Ill. App. 280 (1st D. 1904). However, an attorney who proceeds to question prospective jurors when fewer than twelve are in the box can constitute a waiver of the right. *Oakwood Stock Farm Co. v. Rahn*, 106 Ill. App. 269 (2nd D. 1903).

Usually, outside the twelve jurors in the jury box, the courtroom is filled with additional summoned jurors who are waiting to be seated in the jury box when a prospective juror is deselected by statutory disqualification, hardship, peremptory challenge, or challenge for cause.

2.2. SUPREME COURT RULE 234

In civil cases, Illinois Supreme Court Rule 234, along with the case law interpreting it, controls the voir dire process as follows:

> **The Voir Dire Examination of Prospective Jurors**
>
> The court shall conduct the voir dire examination of prospective jurors by putting to them questions it thinks appropriate touching upon their qualifications to serve as jurors in the case on trial.
>
> The court may permit the parties to submit additional questions to it for further inquiry if it thinks they are appropriate, and
>
> [The court] shall permit the parties to supplement the examination by such direct inquiry as the court deems proper for a reasonable period of time depending upon the length of examination by the court, the complexity of the case, and the nature and extent of the damages.
>
> Questions shall not directly or indirectly concern matters of law or instructions.
>
> The court shall acquaint prospective jurors with the general duties and responsibilities of jurors.
>
> —*amended April 3, 1997, effective May 1, 1997*

Appellate criminal law cases interpreting Rule 234 are good law, applicable in civil voir dire cases.

Until 1997, the same Rule 234 had also been applicable to voir dire in criminal cases. Then, in 1997, the Illinois Supreme Court adopted Rule 431 for voir dire in criminal cases. Nevertheless, appellate criminal law cases interpreting Rule 234 are good law, applicable in civil voir dire cases. *People v. Stack*, 112 Ill. 2d 301 (1986).

2.3. COURT CONDUCTED VOIR DIRE

Rule 234 requires that the court ask the jurors appropriate questions about their qualifications. This inquiry can't be just cursory. It has to be a legitimate interrogation about their backgrounds, experiences, and potential biases.

2.3.a. **The Trial Judge Must Conduct an Adequate Voir Dire Examination**

The trial judge has a duty to conduct voir dire. Illinois Sup.Ct. Rule 234; *Hockett v. Dawdy*, 180 Ill. App.3d 497 (5th D. 1989). The trial judge must conduct some form of voir dire examination so that the parties can select jurors who are qualified, competent, and without bias, prejudice, or partiality. *People v. Lanter*, 230 Ill. App.3d 72, 595 N.E.2d 210 (1992); *Benushka v. Dahl*, 87 Ill. App.3d 911 (2nd D. 1980).

The trial judge has discretion as to the scope and extent of voir dire examination of prospective jurors. *Kingston v. Turner*, 115 Ill. 2d 445, 464–65 (1987); *Limer v. Cassasa*, 273 Ill. App.3d 300, 302 (4th D. 1995). On appeal, the court's inquiry regarding an adequate voir dire examination is whether the trial judge employed procedures and questions which created a reasonable assurance that any bias or prejudice would be discovered. *Friedman v. Park Dist. of Highland Park*, 151 Ill. App.3d 374 (2nd D. 1986); *Limer, Id.*

2.3.b. **Abuse of Discretion Standard**

When the trial judge limits voir dire examination to the broad, all-embracing question of whether the jurors would follow the court's instructions on the law, a party's right to an impartial jury has not been protected. *People v. Stack*, 112 Ill. 2d 301 (1986).

A trial judge's abuse of discretion during voir dire is established when the judge limits supplemental inquiry that denies a party a fair opportunity to properly investigate an area of bias or prejudice among potential jurors. *Thornhill v. Midwest Physician Center of Orland Park*, 337 Ill. App.3d 1034 (1st

D. 2003); *Golden v. Kishwaukee Community Health Services*, 269 Ill. App.3d 37, 645 N.E.2d 319 (1st D. 1995); *Grossman v. Gebarowski*, 315 Ill. App.3d at 222; *People v. Gregg*, 315 Ill. App.3d 59 (2000); *People v. Oliver*, 265 Ill. App.3d 543, 548, 637 N.E.2d 1173 (1994) (judge refused to allow question of whether prospective jurors had been a victim of a crime).

In *Schneider v. Kirk*, 83 Ill. App.2d 170 (1967), prospective jurors merely stating that they can be fair and follow the law did not reasonably allow a party to determine that the juror is not biased or prejudiced toward an issue in the case.

In *People v. Thomas*, 89 Ill. App.3d 592 (1st D. 1980), the trial judge was reversed for refusal to allow further inquiry of prospective jurors based on juror responses suggesting potential bias.

The extent of voir dire that the trial judge should allow is illustrated in the case of *Grossman v. Gebarowski*, 315 Ill. App.3d 213 (1st D. 2000). In *Grossman*, the court reversed a jury verdict in favor of the defendant because the trial court refused to allow the plaintiff's counsel to directly question the jurors during voir dire. The *Grossman* court reviewed the scope and breadth of the trial judge's voir dire examination and concluded that examination was insufficient to ensure an impartial jury.

Specifically, in *Grossman*, the trial judge's voir dire examination included:

- **Nature of the case:** The trial court informed the venire about the nature of the case, the location of the accident, the names of the parties and their counsel, a brief description of the parties' allegations, and the names of potential witnesses.
- **Jurors' backgrounds:** The court questioned each prospective juror, inquiring about each juror's residence, occupation, employer, and marital status; the ages and sex of any children; the occupation of a spouse or ex-spouse, either parent, and any children, in-laws, or siblings; any prior jury service; any involvement in lawsuits; the relationship, if any, to anyone injured or killed in an automobile accident; whether the juror drove; the juror's educational background; any history of cerebral palsy or other disability in the

juror's family background or close set of friends; and whether or not the juror could give both sides a fair trial.

- **Follow-up questions:** If a prospective juror disclosed information in response to the trial court's questions, the court would ask follow-up questions. For example, if a prospective juror disclosed a prior lawsuit and accident history, the court inquired about the nature of both the accident and the injuries sustained, whether a claim had been made, the name of the retained attorney, and the disposition of the claim.
- **Experience of relatives and friends:** If a prospective juror disclosed that a family member or close friend had been involved in an accident, the court asked the juror to describe the nature of the accident and any injuries sustained.
- **Prior claims:** When a prospective juror disclosed that she and her spouse had been injured at work and had filed workers' compensation claims, the court asked whether that experience would prevent the prospective juror from "in any way" giving the parties a fair trial.
- **Connection to disability:** If a prospective juror disclosed any relationship to disabled persons, the court asked further questions to uncover the nature and extent of the disability.

Under *Grossman*, the implication is that if the plaintiff's attorney had been allowed to participate in voir dire, then he would have been permitted to engage thorough exploration of any prospective juror's answers to the trial judge's questions and discover any latent bias. Thus, under *Grossman*, the trial judge is well advised to allow attorney voir dire under Rule 234.

2.4. ATTORNEY CONDUCTED VOIR DIRE

The court may permit the parties to submit additional questions to it for further inquiry if it thinks they are appropriate . . . (Supreme Court Rule 234)

This portion of Rule 234 clearly contemplates attorneys submitting juror questionnaires. In many jurisdictions, the attorneys submit written questions for the jurors to individually answer on sensitive, social, or personal issues similar to what may arise in the courtroom during the trial on the merits. If the jurors answer the questions privately in writing and deliver the questionnaires to the trial judge, then a juror can be questioned in chambers outside the presence of other potential jurors, preventing information from "tainting" the entire venire.

Alternatively, an attorney's well-crafted additional set of questions for jurors which is submitted to the trial judge establishes a record of the nature and scope of voir dire examination necessary in terms of time, liability, and damages. *York v. El-Ganzouri*, 353 Ill. App.3d 1 (1st D. 2004). (The defense attorney objecting to the court's time limitation would have been well served to make an offer of proof in the record of the proposed additional areas of voir dire that were necessary to cover to assure an impartial jury for purposes of appeal.)

2.4.a. **Attorney's Right to Direct Questioning of Prospective Jurors Is Strongly Favored**

> *[The court] shall permit the parties to supplement the examination by such direct inquiry as the court deems proper for a reasonable period of time depending upon the length of examination by the court, the complexity of the case, and the nature and extent of the damages.* (Supreme Court Rule 234)

The Illinois Supreme Court has held that a trial judge should exercise discretion in favor of attorneys conducting direct voir dire examination of jurors. *People v. Garstecki*, 234 Ill. 2d 430 (2009). The attorney's right to conduct direct voir dire is not absolute. In *Garstecki*, while reviewing Rule 431, which is virtually identical to Rule 234, the Illinois Supreme Court held that the change from "may" to "shall" in Rule 431 (same change made in Rule 234) does not make mandatory the direct questioning of jurors by the attorneys. However, the *Garstecki* court agreed that the trial court should exercise discretion strongly in favor of direct attorney questioning of prospective jurors. *Id.*

In the wrongful death auto-pedestrian negligence case of *Grossman v. Gebarowski*, the trial judge was reversed because he did not allow the attorneys to participate in the voir dire examination. 732 N.E.2d 1100 (1st D. 2000). The judge had only allowed written questions to be submitted. *Id.*

The trial attorney would be well served to file a request for attorney conducted voir dire.

2.4.b. **Court's Limitation of Time**

The trial judge can limit the attorneys' time for voir dire under Rule 234. In *York v. El-Ganzouri*, 353 Ill. App.3d 1 (1st D. 2004), the court upheld time limitation, although the defense attorney effectively waived his objection to time limitation and did not perfect a record for appeal.

An attorney objecting to an unreasonable time limitation for voir dire must make a showing in the record by submitting proposed written questions that he would have asked about other pertinent matters or he waives a time restriction objection. *York*, 353 Ill. App.3d 1 (Held: defense attorney's objection to twenty-minute limit to voir dire waived.)

2.5. THE ORDER OF VOIR DIRE

The "jury shall be passed upon in panels of four by the parties, *commencing with the plaintiff.*" 705 ILCS 305/21 (emphasis added); see also, *Collison v. Illinois Central*, 239 Ill. 532 (1909), where the court approved that the plaintiff must proceed first with each panel.

However, under Illinois Supreme Court Rule 233, the court has granted the trial judge the authority to alter the order of jury selection:

> The parties shall proceed at all stages of the trial, including the selection of the prospective jurors as specified in Rule 234 ... in the order in which they appear in the pleadings unless otherwise agreed by all the parties or ordered by the court. (Supreme Court Rule 233)

In *People v. McCormick*, 328 Ill. App.3d 378, 766 N.E.2d 671 (2nd D. 2002), the trial judge's use of a "strike" system for selecting a jury was affirmed. There, the trial judge gave both sides unlimited peremptory challenges. Under Rule 233 and McCormick, a trial judge can alter the manner in which the trial attorney addresses and questions prospective jurors. For example, the trial judge may require the trial attorneys to examine all twelve jurors in the box together, then accept panels of four to comply with the statute. 705 ILCS 305/21.

2.6. JURORS SHALL BE ACCEPTED IN PANELS OF FOUR

By Illinois statute, the jury shall be passed upon in panels of four by the parties. 705 ILCS 305/21.

The plaintiff's attorney goes first in questioning a panel of four and then tenders the panel to the opposing attorney. *Maher v. New York*, 280 Ill. App.222 (1935). Until both sides have accepted a panel of four, either side may exercise a peremptory challenge as to any juror tendered to the other side. *People v. Gray*, 251 Ill. 431 (1911). Even though a party does tender a panel, that side may still exercise its peremptory challenges until both sides have accepted the panel of four. *People v. Murray*, 73 Ill. App.2d 376 (1st D. 1966).

After the panel has been accepted on both sides, if a juror is excused by the court, neither party can exercise a peremptory challenge as to the accepted jurors. *Mayers v. Smith*, 121 Ill. 442 (1887).

When a party breaks a panel by exercising a challenge, that party must examine and pass upon the replacement juror before tendering the panel back to the other side. *People v. Nylin*, 139 Ill. App. 500 (5th D. 1908), *affm'd* 236 Ill. 19 (1908).

2.7. BACK STRIKING

The concept of "back striking" means that a party has the right to challenge a panel that it had previously accepted and tendered to the opposing party, provided, however, that opposing party breaks the accepted panel by removing a juror. *Needy v. Sparks*, 51 Ill. App.3d 350 (1st D. 1977). In civil cases, this right to back striking is of ancient origin and is not affected by Supreme Court Rule 234 providing for the voir dire examination of jurors. *Koester v. Johnson*, 158 Ill. App.3d 747, 511 N.E.2d 262 (4th D. 1987).

The trial court has discretion to alter the usual procedure for exercising peremptory challenges if both parties have adequate notice of the system to be used and the method chosen does not unduly restrict the use of challenges. The trial court may prohibit back striking, where it notified both parties before initiating voir dire and questioned in detail each of the prospective jurors. *People v. Moss*, 108 Ill. 2d 270 (1985).

Because some judges do not approve of back striking, it is important that counsel determine whether back striking will be allowed before an attempt is made to back strike a prospective juror. *People v. Page*, 196 Ill. App.3d 285 (3rd D. 1990).

Once a juror has been both accepted and sworn, neither party has the right to exercise a peremptory challenge by back striking a juror. *People v. Peeples*, 205 Ill. 2d 480, 520 (2002).

2.8. CHOOSING ALTERNATE JURORS

The voir dire process does not necessarily end with the selection of twelve jurors. The Illinois Civil Code of Procedure provides the trial judge with discretion to seat alternate jurors as follows:

Alternate jurors shall be drawn in the same manner, have the same qualifications, be subject to the same examination and challenges, take the same oath, and have the same functions, powers, facilities, and privileges as the principal jurors.

The court may direct that 1 or 2 jurors in addition to the regular panel be impaneled to serve as alternate jurors. Alternate jurors, in the sequence in which they are ordered into the jury box, shall replace jurors who, prior to the time the jury retires to consider its verdict, become unable to perform their duties. Alternate jurors shall be drawn in the same manner, have the same qualifications, be subject to the same examination and challenges, take the same oath, and have the same functions, powers, facilities, and privileges as the principal jurors. An alternate juror who does not replace a principal juror shall be discharged at the time the jury retires to consider its verdict. If alternate jurors are called each side shall be allowed one additional peremptory challenge, regardless of the number of alternate jurors called. The additional peremptory challenge may be used only against an alternate juror, but any unexercised peremptory challenges may be used against an alternate juror. 735 ILCS 5/2-1106(b) (emphasis added).

* * *

Based on the court decisions cited in this chapter, trial attorneys should expect and request sufficient time for voir dire and the right to ask an adequate scope of questions to prospective jurors before they are selected or deselected. Judges now have less discretion on limiting a trial attorney directly questioning prospective jurors. The more the prospective jurors bare their souls about their past experiences and beliefs, the more likely it is that the trial attorney can discover who's really a fair juror and who isn't. The next chapter covers the subject matter and types of questions allowed in voir dire and some prohibitions limiting what trial attorneys may say and do.

ONLINE RESOURCES

TRIAL LAWYERS SHOULD VISIT THE AUTHOR'S WEBSITE AT KURTDLLOYD.COM AND SUBSCRIBE TO HIS BLOG, LLOYD'S TRIAL NOTEBOOK (LLOYDSTRIALNOTEBOOK.COM), TO DOWNLOAD A SAMPLE "MOTION FOR ATTORNEY CONDUCTED VOIR DIRE."

CHAPTER 3: SCOPE OF VOIR DIRE, TYPES OF QUESTIONS ALLOWED

Jurors don't believe what they see, they see what they believe. Jurors listen and perceive the evidence presented and the law given through their belief system. The greatest trial lawyer will not change the juror's belief system. The lawyer can only hope to know a juror's beliefs and meet him where he is. Through voir dire questioning, the trial attorney wants to identify prospective jurors with beliefs that would prevent them from giving the case a fair hearing on the law and anticipated evidence.

Jurors listen and perceive the evidence presented and the law given through their belief system.

The trial lawyer's voir dire questioning should be designed to discover each juror's belief system; that is the lens through which he will evaluate the case. The prospective juror's belief system includes his attitudes toward applicable laws and key evidence, background, education, prior life experiences similar to the facts of the case, and social relationships to the parties or people related or similar to the parties.

In this chapter, the case law is thoroughly set forth, outlined, and explained so that the trial lawyer can draft voir dire questions that will withstand objection and hopefully permit discovery of jurors with negative, biased belief systems. Based on the prospective juror's answers, the trial lawyer can then intelligently move to deselect that juror, either with a peremptory challenge or a cause challenge.

ONLINE RESOURCES

TRIAL LAWYERS SHOULD VISIT THE AUTHOR'S WEBSITE AT KURTDLLOYD.COM AND SUBSCRIBE TO HIS BLOG, LLOYD'S TRIAL NOTEBOOK (LLOYDSTRIALNOTEBOOK.COM), TO DOWNLOAD A "VOIR DIRE WORKBOOK" THAT WILL HELP IN DRAFTING AND ORGANIZING AN EFFECTIVE SET OF VOIR DIRE QUESTIONS FOR THEIR CASE.

3.1. QUESTIONS REGARDING A JUROR'S ATTITUDES TOWARD APPLICABLE LAW OR JURY INSTRUCTIONS

No questions that "directly or indirectly concern matters of law or instructions." (Supreme Court Rule 234)

Despite Illinois Supreme Court Rule 234's proscription against asking a juror questions of law or instructions, Illinois appellate courts have held that attorneys may state to a juror a brief and fair summary of legal principles applicable to the case and then ask if they could apply those principles to the anticipated evidence in the case. *People v. Davis*, 95 Ill. 2d 1, 18 (1983); *People v. Mapp*, 283 Ill. App.3d 979, 989 (1st D. 1996) (a party or his lawyer cannot expect a prospective juror to understand the law before he receives the jury instructions). The Rule 234 proscription against questions of law or instructions is not so narrowly interpreted. *Schaffner v. Chicago Northwestern*, 129 Ill. 2d 1 (1989); *Hartigan v. Robertson*,

87 Ill App.3d 366, 369 (1st D. 1980); *Schneider v. Kirk*, 83 Ill. App.2d 170, 176–77 (1967). An attorney cannot instruct on the law. Neither the trial judge nor attorneys should explain or define legal terms contained in the jury instructions. *Bishop v. Crowther*, 92 Ill. App.3d 1, 11 (1st D. 1980).

An attorney cannot instruct on the law. Neither the trial judge nor attorneys should explain or define legal terms contained in the jury instructions.

However, an attorney can state to a prospective juror a rule of law that is anticipated from the jury instructions and then ask that juror's attitude toward that rule of law. For example, an attorney may inquire as to whether a prospective juror has a disagreement with a particular rule of law that will be applied in that case. *Limer v. Casassa*, 273 Ill. App.3d 300, 302 (4th D. 1995). More specifically, an attorney may ask a prospective juror whether he will follow the court's instructions on the law, ask a juror's ability to understand the law, and particularly ask whether the juror is "reasonably likely" to have a prejudice against a legal principle. *Carter v. Chicago Midland Railway Co.*, 168 Ill. App.3d 652 (4th D. 1988).

For legal issues of intense controversy, the judge or lawyers simply asking jurors whether they could faithfully apply the law as instructed is not enough to reveal juror bias and prejudice toward a rule of law or defense. *People v. Stack*, 112 Ill. 2d 301, 312 (1986). But the trial lawyer cannot question prospective jurors as to extraneous legal principles or concepts that do not bear on whether they are willing to accept and follow the instructions concerning the law of the case. *People v. Stack*, 112 Ill. 2d 301, 311 (1986); *People v. Dow*, 240 Ill. App.3d 392, 396 (1992).

3.1.a. Legal Liability

In any jury trial, a trial lawyer may ask prospective jurors whether they disagree with a particular law. *Limer v. Casassa*, 273 Ill. App.3d 300, 302 (4th D. 1995). *Schneider v. Kirk*, 83 Ill. App.2d 170, 177, 226 N.E.2d 655, 658 (2nd D. 1967) (a party is not adequately protected by a prospective juror's statement that he will follow the law unless the party is certain that the juror knows what the law is governing the case). For example, in a "dram shop" case, the plaintiff's attorney may properly ask jurors whether they have a disagreement with a law that states that when a person is injured by an intoxicated person, the plaintiff may recover from the tavern that served the alcohol. *Schneider*, at 176–77 (1967). (Rule 234's prohibition against questions of law is not intended to prevent inquiry into whether juror might be biased against the law).

3.1.b. **Legal Defenses**

Similarly, courts in Illinois have allowed an attorney's voir dire questions to jurors regarding legal defenses of law as follows:

3.1.b.1. **Contributory Negligence (Plaintiff Conduct)**

The plaintiff's attorney may ask jurors whether they have any disagreement with a law that does not allow for plaintiff's contributory negligence as a defense. *Kirk v. Walter E. Deuchler Associates, Inc.*, 79 Ill. App.3d 416, 424 (2nd D. 1979).

The plaintiff's attorney may also ask prospective jurors about the plaintiff's contributory negligence as a defense. *Grossman v. Gebarowski*, 315 Ill. App.3d 213, 222 (1st D. 2000). In *Grossman*, the plaintiff's counsel, with the express permission of the court, drew the jurors' attention to the fact that this case involved a pedestrian who was struck by an automobile while she was attempting to cross a street in mid-block rather than at a pedestrian crosswalk, and then asked each juror whether there was anything about this situation that might prevent him from viewing the evidence in an open-minded and impartial manner. The *Grossman* court held that plaintiff's attorney is allowed to ask questions sufficient to identify jurors who are biased against a plaintiff who is contributorily negligent—

crossing mid-block (jaywalking) as opposed to at an intersection or crosswalk—under the law of comparative negligence.

3.1.b.2. **Insanity Defense**

In *People v. Stack*, 112 Ill. 2d 301, 312 (1986), holding that a question directed toward a juror's attitude about insanity defense did not violate Rule 234, the Supreme Court approved:

> Do you have any feeling or viewpoint concerning the defense of insanity in a criminal case? If so, what?

The question merely seeks to determine whether a prospective juror would be biased against a law that allows the defendant to claim an insanity defense. *Id.* See also, *People v. Bowel*, 111 Ill. 2d 58, 65 (1986).

3.1.b.3. **Accountability Defense**

In *People v. Davis*, 95 Ill. 2d 1, 18 (1983), regarding the accountability charge for murder, the prosecutor asked two prospective jurors who later were selected:

> The Court will instruct you about this, this aspect of the law, that a person can be held accountable and responsible for the acts of another. Would it affect your ability in deciding this case on the issue or the charge of murder provided that the law states that the defendant could be held accountable under the facts that the defendant, this defendant before you, did not do the direct act, did not pull the trigger of the gun so to speak, that caused the death of the individual. Do you think that would affect your ability to decide or could you follow that law?

The *Davis* court held that the prosecutor did not instruct the jury as to the applicable law. The prosecutor merely inquired as to whether the jurors could follow the law even if the evidence revealed that the defendant did not actually do the shooting. *Davis*, 95 Ill. 2d at 18. This form of voir dire was not error.

Arguably, under *Davis*, a plaintiff lawyer's questions to jurors about liability under laws of agency where the principal did nothing wrong should be allowed.

3.1.c. **Burden of Proof**

In *Schaffner v. Chicago Northwestern*, 129 Ill. 2d 1, 33 (Ill. Sup. Ct. 1989), the Illinois Supreme Court held that it was not error for the trial judge to inform the jury of the difference between a civil plaintiff's burden of proof and criminal prosecution's burden of proof. However, the trial judge or a lawyer must accurately state the "more probably true than not" standard applicable to the civil burden of proof. *Id.*, 33. Any misstatements by the court or attorneys in defining the burden of proof standard, however, are cured by instructing the jury with Illinois Pattern Instructions No. 21.01 on the meaning of the burden of proof. *Id.*

The standard approved Illinois Pattern Instructions No. 21.01 for burden of proof required in a civil trial provides:

> *When I say that a party has the burden of proof on any proposition, or use the expression "if you find," or "if you decide," I mean you must be persuaded, considering all the evidence in the case, that the proposition on which he has the burden of proof is more probably true than not true.*

In *Hartigan v. Robertson*, 87 Ill. App.3d 366, 372 (1st D. 1980), relying on the decision in *Schaffner v. Chicago Northwestern*, 129 Ill. 2d 1 (Ill. Sup. Ct. 1989), the court reasoned that although Rule 234 states that "questions shall not directly or indirectly concern matters of law or instructions," the rule is not so narrowly interpreted. The *Hartigan* court also reasoned that Rule 234 provides that "[t]he court may acquaint prospective jurors with the general duties and responsibilities of jurors." The *Hartigan* court found that the trial judge's comments on the burden of proof were intended to serve that purpose. *Id.*

A trial judge's incorrect statement of law does not prejudice a defendant when the jury is properly instructed on plaintiffs' burden of proof under IPI 21.01 prior to its deliberations. *Hartigan v. Robertson*, 87 Ill. App.3d 366, 369 (1st D. 1980). The trial judge's reference to a "scales of justice" analogy to explain differences between criminal and civil burdens of proof was harmless error because it was cured by the giving IPI Civil 2d No. 21.01. Id., citing *Schaffner v. Chicago Northwestern*, 129 Ill. 2d 1 (Ill. Sup. Ct. 1989).

Similarly, the plaintiff's lawyer did not commit reversible error when he misstated to a prospective juror that the plaintiff's burden of proof was the "greater weight of the evidence" and not "beyond a reasonable doubt." The defendant objected as to plaintiff's lawyer attempting to instruct the jury. The trial judge sustained the defendant's objection *as to the form of the question.* In the appellate court's opinion, Illinois Pattern Instructions No. 1.01, 21.01, and 21.02, all given by the trial court, were sufficient to clarify this situation. *Hartigan v. Robertson*, 87 Ill. App.3d 366, 369, 372 (1st D. 1980). See also, *Heiser v. Chastain*, 6 Ill. App.3d 552 (2nd D. 1972).

Jurors must be informed about the defendant asserting a defense that carries a lesser burden of proof and questioned about their biases or prejudices about that lesser burden. *People v. Gregg*, 315 Ill. App.3d 59, 65, 70, 732 N.E.2d 1152 (1st D. 2000). In *Gregg*, the court concluded that the defendant's right to an impartial jury was diminished when his lawyer could not meaningfully inquire on voir dire about a potential juror's prejudice concerning a lesser burden of proof. *Id.*, at 71.

Inevitably, when the trial judge loads the jury box with twelve jurors, the prospective jurors include a scientist, engineer, accountant, or math or science teacher who lives and works with an absolute certainty standard. These jurors want 100 percent proof that something happened the way the plaintiff lawyer said it did. In jury selection, these jurors should be asked whether they have a quarrel with a law that requires that the plaintiff only prove more probably true than not that a defendant was negligent. For defense lawyers, this same concern can arise when trying to prove that a different conduct caused the injury that the plaintiff is complaining about.

A party is not adequately protected by a prospective juror's statement that he will follow the law unless the party is certain that the juror knows what the law is governing the case. *Schneider v. Kirk*, 83 Ill. App.2d 170, 177, 226 N.E.2d 655, 658 (2nd D. 1967).

Thus, under *Gregg* and *Schneider*, in a civil money damages case a trial lawyer should be able to discuss the differences in the burden of proof between a civil case versus a criminal case so that any misunderstandings or negative juror attitudes toward a lesser burden of proof are revealed.

3.1.d. **Questions Allowed about a Juror's Attitudes toward Credibility of a Witness**

Illinois Pattern Instructions No. 1.01(5) instructs jurors that they shall consider the credibility of a witness. The instruction states:

> *You are the only judges of the credibility of the witnesses. You will decide the weight to be given to the testimony of each of them. In evaluating the credibility of a witness, you may consider that witness' ability and opportunity to observe, memory, manner, interest, bias, qualifications, experience, and any previous inconsistent statement or act by the witness concerning an issue important to the case.*

Based on this jury instruction, a trial lawyer should be able to ask jurors about their attitudes about the credibility of certain witnesses.

3.1.d.1. **Incarcerated Person**

A trial lawyer's questions regarding whether a juror would have bias against the credibility of a witness who is currently incarcerated are allowed. *People v. Smith*, 241 Ill. App.3d 365, 383 (5th D. 1992).

3.1.d.2. **Police Officer**

An attorney is permitted to ask a prospective juror whether he would be more likely to believe a police officer, as opposed to another witness, simply because he was a police officer. *People v. Taylor*, 235 Ill. App.3d 763, 764 (3rd D. 1992).

3.1.d.3. **Victim**

In *People v. Rinehart*, 2012 IL 111719, a prosecutor's questions to prospective jurors were allowed regarding the credibility of the victim because she had delayed reporting her sexual assault. The *Rinehart* court found that because the questions were not based on the specific facts of the case but rather were designed to intelligently assess jurors' beliefs on the credibility of such a victim, such questions were proper.

3.1.e. **Weight of Circumstantial Evidence Versus Eyewitness Testimony**

Illinois Pattern Instructions No. 3.04 instructs jurors on circumstantial evidence. The instruction states:

Circumstantial evidence is entitled to the same consideration as any other type of evidence.

A fact or a group of facts, may, based on logic and common sense, lead you to a conclusion as to other facts. This is known as circumstantial evidence. A fact may be proved by circumstantial evidence. [For example, if you are in a building and a person enters who is wet and is holding an umbrella, you might conclude that it was raining outside.] Circumstantial evidence is entitled to the same consideration as any other type of evidence.

The prosecuting attorney's questions regarding a juror's attitude toward lack of eyewitness testimony, i.e. only proof by circumstantial evidence, is allowed. *People v. Freeman*, 60 Ill. App.3d 794, 799–800 (4th D. 1978). Specifically, the *Freeman* court approved of an attorney's question that asked a prospective juror whether he would be disinclined to convict based on circumstantial evidence. *Id.*

3.2. QUESTIONS ALLOWED RELATING TO A JUROR'S ATTITUDES TOWARD CERTAIN TYPES OF ANTICIPATED EVIDENCE

A party is allowed to ask questions about whether potential facts that are anticipated in evidence may affect his ability to serve as a fair juror, provided, however, that the facts do not become a pre-trying, pre-education hypothetical. *Rub v. Conrail*, 331 Ill. App.3d 692, 771 N.E.2d 1015, 1026 (1st D. 2002); *Grossman v. Gebarowski*, 315 Ill. App.3d 213, 222 (1st D. 2000); *People v. Taylor*, 235 Ill. App.3d 763, 764 (3rd D. 1992). For example, in *People v. Lanter*, 230 Ill. App.3d 72, 76 (1992), the court found that asking prospective jurors a general question about whether they have any biases or prejudices that could affect their ability to be impartial does not reasonably assure that a party will discover prejudice about a basic fact in the case, mainly alcohol consumption. The *Lanter* court stated: "It is unrealistic to expect that any but the most sensitive and thoughtful jurors (frequently those least likely to be biased) will have the personal insight, candor and openness to raise their hands and declare themselves biased." *Id.*

3.2.a. **Questions Allowed about a Juror's Attitudes toward Liability Facts**

In *Rub v. Conrail*, 331 Ill. App.3d 692, 771 N.E.2d 1015, 1026 (1st D. 2002), an automobile-railroad crossing collision case, a trial lawyer's questions were allowed about the jurors' attitudes about the defendant having at the train track crossing only crossbuck signs but no lights or gates.

In *Grossman v. Gebarowski*, 315 Ill. App.3d 213, 222 (1st D. 2000), the plaintiff's lawyer, with the express permission of the court, drew the jurors' attention to the fact that this case involved a pedestrian who was struck by an automobile while she was attempting to cross a street in mid-block rather than at a pedestrian crosswalk and then asked each juror whether there was anything about this situation that might prevent him from viewing the evidence in an open-minded and impartial manner.

3.2.b. **Questions Allowed about a Juror's Attitudes toward Certain Social Beliefs**

3.2.b.1. **Drugs and Alcohol**

If intoxication or impairment is an issue in a case, then the trial lawyer's questions about jurors' attitudes toward drugs and alcohol are proper.

In *People v. Lanter*, 230 Ill. App.3d 72, 73, 75 (4th D. 1992), the court found that intoxication is a sufficiently controversial issue to allow holding the following question proper:

> Do you have any feelings about the use of drugs or alcohol that would affect your ability to serve on this jury, if you heard such testimony?

In *Village of Plainfield v. Nowicki*, 367 Ill. App.3d 522, 523 (3rd D. 1980), the court held proper for a trial lawyer to ask whether jurors drink alcohol socially and, if not, whether they have any moral or religious opinions regarding alcohol.

In a traffic case alleging driving under the influence, the defense lawyer is allowed to ask jurors questions about attitudes toward alcohol or drinking to determine any potential bias. *Benuska v. Dahl*, 87 Ill. App.3d 911 (1980).

3.2.b.2. **Interracial Relationships**

In *People v. Clark*, 278 Ill. App.3d 996, 1004 (1996), the court held that the trial judge did not abuse his discretion when allowing the State to ask whether any of the prospective jurors would be unable to be fair or impartial because some witnesses were involved in interracial relationships. In approving this line of questioning, the *Clark* court observed that people of all races "have strong negative feelings about interracial relationships." *Id.*

3.2.b.3. **Remarriage**

In a wrongful death case, the Supreme Court held that prospective jurors may be told by the judge that a plaintiff has remarried. Beyond this point, however, we believe defendants have no legitimate interest in exploring the jurors' attitudes about the remarriage. *Watson v. Fishbach*, 54 Ill. 2d 498, 503. However, the defendant has a right to know of any relationship of the new spouse or her family to prospective jurors. *Id.*

3.2.b.4. **Tort Reform**

In *Limer v. Cassasa*, 273 Ill. App.3d 300 (1992), although the trial judge's refusal to allow questions about tort reform was not error, the court found the following questions on tort reform were not particularly objectionable:

Since the time of the last political conventions up to the present, there has been much discussion in the press and media about health-care reform, legal reform, jury trials, etc.

Do you have any quarrel with the jury system as a way of resolving disputes between parties?

Do you believe in the jury trial system as a legitimate method for our society, through the voice of twelve members of the community, to decide issues when parties are unable to agree?

Importantly, once attorney voir dire is granted, the trial judge does not have to allow questions that raise extraneous legal principles or concepts, which do not relate to the law or instructions of the case. *Limer v. Cassasa*, 273 Ill. App.3d 300, 302 (4th D. 1995) (trial court affirmed for refusing to allow questions as to their beliefs about tort reform), citing *People v. Stack*, 112 Ill. 2d 301, 311 (1986).

3.2.b.5. **Religious Beliefs or Affiliation**

A trial lawyer's questions about religious beliefs can be properly restricted or excluded. *Duncan v. Petersen*, 408 Ill. App.3d 911, 947 N.E.2d 305 (2d D. 2010). Nonetheless, the *Duncan* court agreed that if religion were relevant to potential prejudice, then subjects related to religious affiliation are proper for inquiry. *Id.*, at 923. However, because plaintiff and defendant were both Christian ministers, questions regarding religious beliefs would not have revealed bias toward one side or another. *Id.*

But in *Congregation of the Passion v. Touche Ross & Co.*,159 Ill. 2d 137 (1994), the trial lawyer's questions about religious beliefs were allowed.

In *Turner v. Wallace*, 71 Ill. App.2d 160 (3rd D. 1966), the trial lawyer's questions regarding a prospective juror's preconceived religious or philosophical beliefs regarding pain were allowed.

3.3. QUESTIONS RELATING TO FINANCIAL MATTERS

3.3.a. Questions Prohibited Regarding Financial Matters

3.3.a.1. Wealth or Poverty of a Party

Any attorney questions regarding or implying the wealth or poverty of a party are improper. *Brandel v. Yellow Cab Co.*, 98 Ill. App.3d 88 (1st D. 1981).

3.3.a.2. Size of Attorney's Law Firm Representing a Party

Attorney question that makes reference to the size of a law firm is improper. *Friedland v. Allis Chalmers*, 159 Ill. App.3d 1 (1st D. 1987).

3.3.a.3. Source of Funds (Collateral Source)

An attorney may not ask questions that make reference to the source of payment of any verdict or judgment. For example, in a condemnation case, reference to payment for land from city taxpayer bonds was improper. *City of Quincy v. V.E. Best Plumbing*, 17 Ill. 2d 570 (1959).

3.3.a.4. Party's Prior Settlements Disallowed

Trial attorney questions that make reference to a prior partial settlement by plaintiff with a Covenant Not to Execute was improper. *Burger v. Van Severn*, 39 Ill. App.2d 205 (2nd D. 1963).

3.3.a.5. **Insurance**

The direct reference to insurance of a party is reversible error. Plaintiff's attorney cannot inject insurance coverage directly into the case. *Ross v. Aryan International, Inc.*, 219 Ill. App.3d 634, 643 (1st D. 1991); *Imparato v. Rooney*, 95 Ill. App.3d 11, 15 (1st D. 1991).

3.3.b. **Questions Allowed Regarding Financial Matters**

3.3.b.1. **Reference to Award Not Being a Second Recovery (Collateral Source)**

On voir dire, in *Gowler v. Ferrell-Ross*, 206 Ill. App.3d 194, 205 (1st D. 1990), the plaintiff's attorney asked:

> The great principle of law that applies to this case and applies to every case in the courthouse is called the principle against double recovery. There is nobody in this courthouse that ever gets money twice. Nobody that is running this system is going to reward this plaintiff the second or the third time for damages that he received. He's only entitled to one set of damages.
>
> Now, can you follow that principle in this case and not speculate outside the case whether or not by you doing your job on the damages, listening to the instructions, giving him what you know the evidence in the case warrants and requires and not speculate outside that maybe you're now giving him a second recovery. Do you think you can do that?

The *Gowler* court held that the question was proper and not prejudicial grounds for reversal. The *Gowler* court found that plaintiff's counsel's comment was factually correct and, further, that the defendant failed to indicate how counsel's comments prejudiced him. *Gowler* 206 Ill. App.3d 194, 205 (1st D. 1990).

3.3.b.2. **Juror's Relationship to Insurance Industry**

Jurors may be questioned during voir dire as to their possible connection to or interest in an insurance company when this information is necessary for the intelligent exercise of the right of peremptory challenge and is sought in good faith. *Haymes v. Catholic Bishop of Chicago*, 41 Ill. 2d 336 (1969); *Kavanaugh v. Parret*, 379 Ill. 273; *Wheeler v. Rudek*, 397 Ill. 438 (1947); *Seyferlich v. Maxwell*, 28 Ill. App.2d 471 (1st D. 1961); *Moore v. Edmonds*, 384 Ill. 535 (1943).

However, the trial attorney asking a voir dire question about a juror's relationship to insurance usually is in follow-up to a juror's response suggesting an issue of bias based on insurance. For example, in *Saad v. Shimano American Corp.* 2000 US Dist. LEXIS 10974, 2000 WL1063253 (N.D. Ill. July 24, 2000), No. 98 C 1204, the court disallowed the voir dire question of whether venire members or any of their relatives or friends work or have worked in the insurance claims or claims-handling business. The *Saad* court reasoned that the proposed questions likely would suggest to jurors the presence of insurance coverage. The *Saad* court also reasoned that the standard voir dire questioning on employment experience and involvement in lawsuits by prospective jurors and their family members would likely uncover much of the information being sought.

In *Seldin v. Babendir*, the plaintiff's attorney asked:

> Does anybody in this group have any friends or relatives that are lawyers, claims investigators, insurance adjusters, anybody involved in these actions?

The *Seldin* court held direct inquiry about insurance improper, although harmless error. *Seldin*, 325 Ill. App.3d 1058, 1066, 759 N.E.2d 28, 37 (1st D. 2001). However, the *Seldin* court did not state that it is improper to ask jurors about prior employment. Such questions about prior employment may spontaneously reveal insurance relationship.

The mere mention of the word "insurance" during a personal injury trial does not require a per se declaration of a mistrial. *Neyelman v. Treitman*, 95 Ill. App.3d 511 (1st D. 1995).

The mere mention of the word "insurance" during a personal injury trial does not require a per se declaration of a mistrial.

3.3.c. Juror's Prior Personal Injury Claims or Accidents

3.3.c.1. Juror's Experience with Personal Injury Claims and Attitude about No Settlement

In *Cummings v. CTA*, 86 Ill. App.3d 919 (1st D. 1980), after a juror stated experience with a prior personal injury case and settlement, the plaintiff's lawyer informed the juror that the plaintiff was unable to settle his case and then was permitted to ask the juror whether the juror would be influenced by the fact that the instant case had not been settled.

The *Cummings* court held that in view of the circumstances, nothing was improper about the question. Either party was entitled to expose any latent bias or prejudice of the prospective juror about a previous personal injury claim or settlement. The trial lawyer's question did not connote or indoctrinate the panel to believe that the defendant was guilty of any wrongdoing, nor did the question attempt to place the prospective juror in the shoes of the plaintiff.

In *Newlin v. Foresman*, 103 Ill. App.3d 1038, 1047 (1st D. 1982), the plaintiff lawyer's inquiries to jurors about ever being involved in auto accidents, and if so, if they were involved in litigation or made a "claim" as a result of the accident were not improper and did not inject insurance into the case.

3.3.c.2. **Juror's Attitude about Personal Fault in His Own Prior Accident**

In *Friedman v. Park Dist. of Highland Park,* 151 Ill. App.3d 374 (2nd D. 1986), the defendant's lawyer asked a juror who had a prior sledding accident: "Do you think your striking the curb was the fault of the City of Dubuque or did your own lack of care have something to do with it?"

An objection as to indoctrination was overruled. In the instant case, the previous involvement of a potential juror in a sledding accident would serve as a key area for scrutiny by both parties regarding possible preconceptions of that juror. The standard for evaluating whether the trial court has abused its discretion in the questioning of jurors is whether the inquiry creates a reasonable assurance that prejudice would be discovered if present. The *Friedman* court held that the question posed here was proper when measured by this standard. Further, the determination of whether or not a juror is qualified lies with the trial court and must be made on the evidence, not on a mere suspicion of undue influence. *Id.*

TWO CASES, DIFFERENT RULINGS INVOLVING FACT-RELATED QUESTIONS

In *Dixson v. University of Chicago Hospitals*, 190 Ill. App.3d 369 (1st D. 1989), the plaintiff's lawyer told the prospective jurors that the case involved professional negligence and that "there might be some evidence against nurses..." Then the plaintiff's lawyer asked the jurors if they would have any hesitance in awarding damages if the plaintiff proved her case, even though they might have relatives or friends who were nurses.

The trial judge instructed the plaintiff's lawyer to stop telling the jurors what he thought the evidence would show and what the plaintiff would ask for at the end of the trial.

Plaintiff's lawyer argued that he had a right to ask those questions because all the prospective jurors had revealed a connection to a hospital or nurse, therefore he should be allowed to determine whether that connection might affect their judgment, inasmuch as he was asking for a verdict based on the professional negligence of a nurse. The trial judge refused to allow the plaintiff's lawyer to continue his line of questioning, stating that the trial court had already asked the jury venire the same questions.

The *Dixson* court held it was not reversible error because the jurors stated they could be fair after the jurors heard the plaintiff's lawyer question a juror who admitted she might be biased and also saw that she was excused for that bias. *Dixson v. Univ. of Chicago Hospitals*, 190 Ill. App.3d 369, 377 (1st D. 1989).

But a trial lawyer's questions to potential jurors about opinions on the types of railroad crossing protection they believed were appropriate based on some anticipated evidence were upheld in *Rub v. Conrail*, 331 Ill. App.3d 692, 771 N.E.2d 1015, 1026 (1st D. 2002). Plaintiff's lawyer had objected to such questions as no evidence had yet been presented. The court found that the questions "were appropriately designed to expose any latent prejudice by jurors against railroad crossings where no lights, gates, or flashers were present."

3.4. QUESTIONS RELATING TO TYPES AND EXTENT OF DAMAGES

3.4.a. Questions Allowed about a Juror's Attitudes toward Money Damages for Pain But Not about Personal Experience with Pain

The court-approved money damages instruction that a jury receives in any injury cases provides:

> If you decide for the plaintiff on the question of liability, you must then fix the amount of money which will reasonably and fairly compensate him for any of the following elements of damages proved by the evidence to have resulted from the negligence of the defendant, taking into consideration the nature, extent and duration of the injury.
>
> The pain and suffering experienced and reasonably certain to be experienced in the future as a result of the injuries.
>
> Loss of a normal life experienced (and reasonably certain to be experienced in the future).
>
> The disfigurement resulting from the injury.
>
> Whether any of these elements of damages has been proved by the evidence is for you to determine. I.P.I. 30.01

In *Turner v. Wallace*, 71 Ill. App.2d 160, 172 (3rd D. 1966), the plaintiff's lawyer asked a prospective juror who had worked in a doctor's office whether she "had ever experienced pain." Sustaining the defendant's objection, the Turner court ruled that a juror cannot be asked to step into the shoes of the plaintiff regarding pain experienced. The plaintiff's lawyer argued that some people "stoically believe there is no pain or that it is not compensable" and that the ruling of the trial court prevented him from pertinent inquiry to ascertain the jurors' state of mind, so that his right of peremptory challenge could be exercised intelligently. The *Turner* court found that the plaintiff's lawyer could have ascertained the juror's attitudes toward pain by specifically asking the juror about her attitudes toward pain rather than her experiences; therefore, the trial judge sustaining the objection did not deprive the plaintiff of a pertinent inquiry. *Id.*, at 172–3. The *Turner* court held that the voir dire did not prohibit counsel from inquiring about a prospective juror's attitudes. *Id.*

3.4.b. **Questions Allowed Regarding a Juror's Attitudes toward Specific Dollar Amounts**

The plaintiff's lawyer is permitted to ask the prospective jurors whether they could award "two million dollars" if it were proved under the law and the evidence to be an appropriate amount. *Kinsey v. Kolber*, 103 Ill. App.3d 933, 943 (1st D. 1982).

The plaintiff lawyer's inquiries to jurors about whether "a figure of $600,000" was a figure that they "could not possibly consider under any circumstances," "would scare them," or would be "too much money for anybody" was held not indoctrination but rather was designed to expose latent bias against large verdicts. *Scully v. Otis Elevator Co.,* 2 Ill. App.3d 185, 198 (1st D. 1971).

The trial judge does have some discretion, however, concerning whether the plaintiff's lawyer is allowed to ask about specific amounts so that he can determine whether a juror has fixed opinions indicating bias toward large verdicts. *Kern v. Uregas*, 90 Ill. App.3d 182, 201–202 (1st D. 1980). See also, *Juarez v. Commonwealth Medical Records*, 318 Ill. App.3d 380 (1st D. 2000), where the court found that it was not reversible error to bar the plaintiff's lawyer from asking prospective jurors if they could sign a verdict for two million dollars.

3.4.c. **Questions Allowed about a Juror's Ability to Award Large Dollar Amounts**

Similarly, preconditioning objections by the defendant were properly overruled as to plaintiff lawyer's questions to jurors about being able to return an award of "very substantial damages." *Wells v. Web Machinery Co.*, 20 Ill. App.3d 545, 554–55 (1st D. 1974). A plaintiff lawyer's question to prospective jurors about whether they would be willing to award a "large" verdict was held proper. *Mack v. Anderson*, 371 Ill. App.3d 36 (1st D. 2006). The appellate court has also approved a plaintiff lawyer's question about whether the jurors could sign a verdict "in the millions." *DeYoung v. Alpha Construction Co.*, 186 Ill. App.3d 758, 764 (1st D. 1989).

However, the plaintiff's lawyer may not frame the question about awarding a specific amount of damages in such a manner as to try to obtain a pledge from a juror. *Juarez v. Commonwealth Medical Records*, 318 Ill. App.3d 380 (1st D. 2000). If the trial judge believes that the inquiry about a specific amount of damages is being used as a form of indoctrination, the lawyer's question may be found improper. *Kinsey v. Kolber*, 103 Ill. App.3d 933, 946–47 (1st D. 1982); *Murphy v. Lindahl*, 24 Ill. App.2d 461 (1st D. 1960).

3.4.d. **Punitive Damages**

A lawyer's questions about juror attitudes concerning the law of punitive damages are allowed, provided, however, that punitive damages have been allowed in the case. *Gomez v. The Finishing Line*, 316 Ill. App.3d 711, 714 (1st D. 2006).

3.4.e. **Sympathy toward the Plaintiff's Injuries**

Illinois Pattern Instructions No. 1.01(3) instructs jurors not to consider sympathy. Specifically, the instruction states:

> *[3] It is your duty to resolve this case by determining the facts based on the evidence and following the law given in the instructions. Your verdict must not be based upon speculation, prejudice, or sympathy. [Each party, whether a [(i.e., corporation, partnership, etc.)] or an individual, should receive your same fair consideration.] . . .*

This instruction is given in every jury trial. A trial lawyer is allowed to ask jurors whether certain evidence, e.g. physical or visual evidence of injury, would create sympathy toward a party, which would prevent them from being fair to both sides. *Roberts v. Sisters of St. Francis*, 198 Ill. App.3d 891 (1st D. 1990). In *Roberts*, the defendant's lawyer was allowed to show a "day in the life" video to prospective jurors and then ask if their sympathies toward the injured plaintiff would prevent them from being fair.

However, in *Foley v. Fletcher*, 361 Ill. App.3d 39 (1st D. 2005), the court held that it is not error for a trial court to refuse to show such a film if the defendants are not otherwise prevented from effectively testing the potential jurors' views on the plaintiff's disabilities for bias or prejudice. If the record of voir dire proceedings does not show that the defendants were unable to question potential jurors thoroughly on the question of the plaintiff's disability, then the trial court did not abuse its discretion in barring the use of a "day in the life" video.

In *Golden v. Kishwaukee Community Health Services Center, Inc.*, 269 Ill. App.3d 37 (1st D. 1994), the court observed that the *Roberts* case allows the trial court discretion to have a "day in the life" video shown to a prospective jury but that the Roberts case does not hold that the video must be shown to a jury.

3.5. SEARCHING JURORS ON THE INTERNET DURING VOIR DIRE

Today, the majority of prospective jurors have some Internet presence, such as a social media account on Google Plus, Facebook, LinkedIn, or Twitter. Many trial lawyers have begun to search for information about prospective jurors posted or available on the Internet. It could be called "Internet voir dire." For example, a prospective juror's LinkedIn page may provide information about employment history, education, training, and job responsibilities that is considerably more extensive than the basic background information provided on the juror card he completed when summoned. A juror's Facebook page may reveal his opinions on social, political, or legal issues, which could shed light on the juror's true background and beliefs. A juror's Facebook page may be as revealing as the bumper sticker on his automobile. Further, many Internet services also can be used to search a prospective juror's litigation history and criminal and traffic records and then compare the records to what the prospective juror has disclosed on his juror card.

In Illinois, an appellate court has yet to decide, as of this book's publication, whether and to what extent such Internet searches are proper for purposes of jury selection and how a trial lawyer can ethically perform such searches without communicating with a prospective juror. However, the American Bar Association has issued formal Opinion 466 outlining ethical limitations on researching prospective jurors on the Internet. In summary, Opinion 466 provides:

- An attorney may not make an "access request" to a prospective juror. This constitutes a communication with the juror which is prohibited.
- If an attorney who through Internet research makes a prospective juror aware that he is reviewing the juror's Internet presence, then such awareness does not constitute a communication.

Thus, under Rule 466 a trial lawyer or his office can research a prospective juror using the Internet and the juror can become aware of it, but the lawyer cannot ask the juror to access his social media accounts. No "friending." A word of caution is in order: An Illinois court could rule in the future that an attorney who makes a prospective juror aware of a review of his social media information constitutes unlawful communication. Further, if the trial lawyer or his office is performing Internet research on prospective jurors while in the courtroom during jury selection, the trial judge could prohibit it or find it an improper form of voir dire examination under Supreme Court Rules 233 and 234, which grant the trial judge authority over the conduct of voir dire. In *Carino v. Muen Zeim*, 2010 WL 3448071 (N.J. App.Div.), the New Jersey Appellate Court has held that the trial judge could prohibit an attorney from Internet research of prospective jurors during jury selection while in the courtroom based on lack of notice to the court and opposing party.

Lastly, a trial lawyer should consider that if a prospective juror who is later selected learns that he was researched on the Internet, then he may feel somehow violated and any rapport or trust built in the voir dire process may be lost.

3.6. USING SUPPLEMENTAL JUROR QUESTIONNAIRES DURING VOIR DIRE

In addition to the questions that prospective jurors are posed on the juror card, an experienced trial lawyer may wish to prepare a supplemental juror questionnaire that he asks the trial judge to distribute to the prospective jurors once they have arrived in the courtroom. In Illinois, no appellate decision or Supreme Court rule addresses the use of a supplemental juror questionnaire. However, nothing in Supreme Court Rule 234 prohibits a trial judge from distributing a written supplemental questionnaire to prospective jurors, particularly where a trial lawyer believes that there is a sensitive or controversial fact issue in the case that jurors would be reluctant to discuss orally during voir dire questioning but could answer privately to the court in writing in a supplemental questionnaire.

For example, in a personal injury automobile collision case involving consumption of alcohol and intoxication, a trial lawyer may wish to know if a prospective juror has ever been arrested or convicted for driving while under the influence. Obviously, potential embarrassment is spared, and a prospective juror is much more likely to disclose this personal information on a written questionnaire, provided that the juror knows the information shall remain confidential between the trial judge and the respective lawyers. The trial lawyer and the judge can then conduct voir dire questioning of such a juror in the judge's chambers. Therefore, for a myriad of controversial or sensitive factual issues, before voir dire begins, a trial lawyer should consider presenting a motion to the trial judge requesting that a supplemental written questionnaire be issued to the prospective jurors, arguing that a supplemental written questionnaire is more likely to discover relevant, perhaps prejudicial, information from some jurors so that hidden, biased jurors are deselected.

3.7. ATTORNEY ADVOCATING THROUGH VOIR DIRE QUESTIONING PROHIBITED

3.7.a. No Pre-Arguing the Case during Voir Dire

A trial lawyer may not ask prospective jurors questions that are tailored to the facts of the case and intended to serve as his preliminary closing argument. *People v. Bowel*, 111 Ill. 2d 58, 64 (1986); *People v. Mapp*, 283 Ill. App.3d 979, 989–90 (1st D. 1996). This means that the trial lawyer during voir dire cannot argue the facts of his case or try to indoctrinate or precondition jurors to his theory of the case.

3.7.b. **No Attempts to Indoctrinate Jurors**

A trial lawyer should object to voir dire questions by the opposing lawyer that are being used "to indoctrinate or pre-educate jurors." *Rub v. Conrail*, 331 Ill. App.3d 692, 696 (1st D. 2002); *Christian v. New York Central Railroad Co.*, 28 Ill. App.2d 57, 67 (4th D. 1960). (The plaintiff's personal injury verdict was reversed because the trial court allowed numerous questions of jurors regarding opinions based on certain assumed evidence or jury instructions. The plaintiff's trial lawyer during voir dire was improperly allowed to indoctrinate, persuade, and control.)

In *People v. Bell*, 152 Ill. App.3d 1007, 1017, 505 N.E.2d 365 (1987), the court found that the prosecuting attorneys' questions were improper because they primarily served to indoctrinate the jurors as to the State's theory of the case and ask the jurors to prejudge the facts of the case.

Similarly, in *People v. Boston*, 383 Ill. App.3d 352, 358, 893 N.E.2d 677 (2008), the court found that prosecutor's voir dire questions were improper because they highlighted factual details about the case and asked the prospective jurors to prejudge the case.

But distinguishing *Bell* and *Boston*, the Illinois Supreme Court in *People v. Rinehart*, 2012 IL 111719 found that the prosecutor's questions were acceptable regarding whether a sexual assault victim's delay in reporting the assault to others would bias jurors' views of the victim's credibility. P. 21. The *Rinehart* court found that the questions were less fact driven and were brief and more general in nature. *Id.* The trial court does not abuse its discretion by allowing questions that create a reasonable assurance of discovering bias. Specifically, the prosecutor's questions regarding delay in reporting the assault were designed to find out if jurors would give less credibility to the victim's testimony, so that the prosecutor could intelligently decide to use a peremptory challenge. *Id.*

In an admitted liability case, the trial lawyer's questions suggesting that the defendant was hiding certain evidence were improper. *Kizinger v. Tull*, 770 N.E.2d 247 (4th D. 2002).

3.8. NO ATTEMPTS TO OBTAIN A PLEDGE FOR A VERDICT FROM JURORS

A trial lawyer should object to an opposing lawyer's attempts to obtain a pledge from prospective jurors about how they will decide the case under a given set of facts. *Rub v. Conrail*, 331, Ill. App.3d 692, 696 (1st D. 2002); *Gowler v. Ferrell-Ross,* 206 Ill. App.3d 199, 207 (1st D. 1990).

In *People v. M.D.*, 231 Ill. App.3d 176, 197 (1992), the trial judge erred when he allowed prosecutors to repeatedly ask prospective jurors whether hearing two versions of events would automatically create reasonable doubt in their minds.

Once voir dire by the trial lawyers is granted, the trial judge does not have to allow questions that raise extraneous legal principles or concepts that do not relate to the law or instructions of the case. *Limer v. Cassasa*, 273 Ill. App.3d 300, 302 (4th D. 1995) (trial court affirmed for refusing to allow questions as to their beliefs about tort reform, citing *People v. Stack*, 112 Ill. 2d 301, 311 (1986)).

* * *

The more the trial lawyer is familiar with the information covered in this chapter about the scope and types of voir dire questions that are allowed, the better the opportunity to find out the juror's true attitudes and beliefs. The next step is to act on that knowledge by bringing appropriate motions in limine to assure that the court will permit the fullest possible questioning.

ONLINE RESOURCES

TRIAL LAWYERS SHOULD VISIT THE AUTHOR'S WEBSITE AT KURTDLLOYD.COM AND SUBSCRIBE TO HIS BLOG, LLOYD'S TRIAL NOTEBOOK (LLOYDSTRIALNOTEBOOK.COM), TO DOWNLOAD A COPY OF "VOIR DIRE WORKBOOK" THAT WILL HELP IN DRAFTING AND ORGANIZING AN EFFECTIVE SET OF VOIR DIRE SUBJECT MATTER QUESTIONS FOR THEIR CASE.

CHAPTER 4: MOTIONS IN LIMINE RELATING TO VOIR DIRE

Too often, trial judges limit the nature and extent of voir dire, which deprives the trial lawyer of necessary information about prospective jurors. Before jury selection begins, a lawyer should consider and prepare motions in limine that establish or exclude areas of juror examination. These motions were not common historically but are becoming a regular practice among skilled trial lawyers. In fact, a skilled trial lawyer often submits proposed questions, which together with the motions is a way of educating the judge about the nature and extent of voir dire that should be allowed.

In all cases, the litigants are entitled to an impartial panel of jurors who are free from bias or prejudice. *Kingston v. Turner*, 115 Ill. 2d 445, 464 (1987). Voir dire serves the dual purpose of enabling the trial court to select jurors who are free from bias or prejudice and ensuring that the trial lawyers have an informed and intelligent basis on which to exercise their peremptory challenges. The right to a jury trial guarantees a fair trial by a panel of impartial jurors.

In a civil injury and damages case, the plaintiff's lawyer should present to the judge a motion in limine, for a ruling from the trial judge granting the parties the following:

4.1. SUFFICIENT TIME TO CONDUCT VOIR DIRE

The limitation of voir dire questioning may constitute reversible error where such limitation denies a party a fair opportunity to probe an important area of potential bias or prejudice among prospective jurors. *People v. Gregg*, 315 Ill. App.3d 29 (1st D. 2000) (citations omitted).

4.2. LATITUDE IN QUESTIONING REGARDING JURORS' OPINIONS, ATTITUDES, BELIEFS

The previous chapter covered the scope and content of voir dire permitted in various areas of applicable law, jury instructions, types of evidence, and social beliefs that may be involved in the facts of a case. A trial lawyer may file a motion in limine to have voir dire explore jurors' opinions, attitudes, and beliefs regarding:

- personal injury claims and lawsuits;
- tort reform and limits on money damages;
- awarding money for pain and suffering, disability, loss of normal life, and disfigurement;
- distinguishing the burden of proof in a civil case versus a criminal case;
- disagreements with rules of law or instructions applicable to case;
- attitudes toward drugs and alcohol (if involved in facts or defense); and
- specific amount of money damages if case is proven.

Several courts in Illinois have recognized that the purpose of voir dire is not only to develop information that can be used to allow challenges for cause but also to allow the trial lawyers to *intelligently exercise* peremptory challenges. See *Schneider v. Kirk*, 83 Ill. App.2d 170, 226 N.E.2d 55 (2nd D. 1967), where the court held it was not intended to prevent counsel from making pertinent inquiries to determine whether a juror might be prejudiced or biased, or to preclude counsel from "intelligently exercising his right of challenge for sufficient cause or peremptorily." An abuse of discretion will be found if, after reviewing the record, it is determined that the judge's conduct thwarted the selection of an impartial jury. *Kingston v. Turner*, 115 Ill. 2d 445 (1987).

On voir dire, an attorney has the right to make such reasonable pertinent inquiries as will permit an intelligent exercise of a right to challenge. *Schneider, supra*; *Watson v.*

Fischbach, 6 Ill. App.3d 166, 284 N.E.2d 720 (1972). In *People v. Lobb*, 17 Ill. 2d 287 (1973), the court found that a failure to permit additional pertinent inquiries by the respective parties to enable such parties to ascertain whether the minds of the jurors are free from bias or prejudice that would constitute a basis of challenge for cause or that would enable them to exercise their right of peremptory challenge intelligently may constitute reversible error. *Street v. Finney*, 9 Ill. App.3d 638 (4th D. 1973).

4.3. COMMON MISUNDERSTANDINGS OF THE CIVIL BURDEN OF PROOF STANDARD

Prospective jurors sometimes think that the plaintiff has a burden of absolute proof or proof beyond a reasonable doubt before there is negligence. Jurors may get this mistaken idea from television dramas. Of course, in a civil case, proof of the plaintiff's theory needs only to be a little more right than wrong.

With this in mind, the plaintiff lawyers should file a motion in limine requesting permission to discuss the difference in proof between a civil and criminal case. The motion can further ask the trial judge to explain to the prospective jurors before voir dire commences that this is a civil trial and the plaintiff's burden of proof is a standard of "more probably true than not true." (See Illinois Pattern Instructions No. 21.01 for burden of proof required in a civil trial quoted previously in Section 3.1.c.) Provided this instruction is given later, the trial judge is allowed to explain that this is not a criminal case and the plaintiff is not required to prove his case beyond a reasonable doubt. *Hartigan v. Robertson*, 87 Ill. App.3d 372 (1st D. 1980).

ONLINE RESOURCES

TRIAL LAWYERS SHOULD VISIT THE AUTHOR'S WEBSITE AT KURTDLLOYD.COM AND SUBSCRIBE TO HIS BLOG, LLOYD'S TRIAL NOTEBOOK (LLOYDSTRIALNOTEBOOK.COM), TO DOWNLOAD A SAMPLE "MOTION FOR ATTORNEY CONDUCTED VOIR DIRE," WHICH INCLUDES THE VOIR DIRE SUBJECT MATTER QUESTIONS DISCUSSED IN THIS CHAPTER.

Under the case law, a trial lawyer is allowed to discuss any disagreements that a prospective juror might have with a law or instructions in the case. As discussed in Section 3.1.c., an attorney should be able to inquire about a potential juror's prejudice regarding a lesser burden of proof. *People v. Gregg*, 315 Ill. App.3d 59, 65, 70, 732 N.E.2d 1152 (1st D. 2000); *Schneider v. Kirk*, 83 Ill. App.2d 170, 177, 226 N.E.2d 655, 658 (2nd D. 1967).

4.4. JUROR ATTITUDES TOWARD AWARDING MONEY FOR PAIN AND SUFFERING, LOSS OF A NORMAL LIFE, AND DISFIGUREMENT

In a civil jury trial, the jurors shall be instructed that the plaintiff is entitled to an award of noneconomic damages for injuries suffered, including pain and suffering, loss of a normal life, and disfigurement. Of course, pain cannot be seen. It is subjective. Some jurors wrestle with giving money for an injury that they cannot see. Other prospective jurors know someone—a relative, a friend of a friend who experiences pain every day—but no one is going to award them any money for pain.

In Illinois, the law allows for a jury awarding noneconomic damages, damages that are intangible, which cannot be seen.

The approved jury instruction regarding money damages in any injury cases provides:

> *If you decide for the plaintiff on the question of liability, you must then fix the amount of money which will reasonably and fairly compensate him for any of the following elements of damages proved by the evidence to have resulted from the negligence of the defendant, taking into consideration the nature, extent and duration of the injury.*
>
> *The pain and suffering experienced and reasonably certain to be experienced in the future as a result of the injuries.*
>
> *Loss of a normal life experienced (and reasonably certain to be experienced in the future).*
>
> *The disfigurement resulting from the injury.*

Whether any of these elements of damages has been proved by the evidence is for you to determine. I.P.I. 30.01

The plaintiff's trial lawyer needs to know if a prospective juror has trouble with or disagrees with a law that instructs that an injured plaintiff is entitled to money for pain and suffering. Thus, the plaintiff's lawyer should bring a motion in limine in advance of voir dire, requesting permission to discuss with prospective jurors their attitudes toward the law of noneconomic damages.

4.5. DEFENSE SHOWING A "DAY IN THE LIFE" VIDEO TO PROSPECTIVE JURORS

Defense lawyers often want to show prospective jurors a "day in the life" video that depicts a catastrophically injured plaintiff and try to eliminate jurors who will be sympathetic to the plaintiff. The Illinois Pattern Instructions No. 1.01(3) instructs jurors not to consider sympathy. Specifically, the instruction states:

[3] It is your duty to resolve this case by determining the facts based on the evidence and following the law given in the instructions. Your verdict must not be based upon speculation, prejudice, or sympathy. [Each party, whether a [(i.e., corporation, partnership, etc.)] or an individual, should receive your same fair consideration.] . . .

This instruction is given in every jury trial. In addition to this part of the Instruction, a defense lawyer may cite *Roberts v. Sisters of St. Francis*, 198 Ill. App.3d 891 (1st D. 1990), for the right to show to the prospective jury the plaintiff's demonstrative "day in the life" video evidence and then ask jurors whether the plaintiff's injuries as depicted would create sympathy toward the plaintiff, which would prevent them from being fair. Specifically, in Roberts, the defendant's attorney was allowed to show a "day in the life" video to prospective jurors and then ask if their sympathies toward the injured plaintiff would prevent them from being fair.

However, the plaintiff's lawyer desiring to block this defense strategy may wish to file a motion in limine, which seeks to prevent the defense from showing a "day in the life" video during jury selection based on the case of *Foley v. Fletcher*, 361 Ill. App.3d 39 (1st D. 2005). There, the *Foley* court held that it is not error for a trial court to refuse to show such a film if the defendants are not otherwise prevented from effectively testing the potential jurors' views on the plaintiff's disabilities for bias or prejudice. If the record of voir dire proceedings does not show that the defendants were unable to question potential jurors thoroughly on the question of the plaintiff's disability, then the trial court did not abuse its discretion in barring the use of a "day in the life" film. As further support, the plaintiff's lawyer should cite *Golden v. Kishwaukee Community Health Services Center, Inc.*, 269 Ill. App.3d 37 (1st D. 1994), where the court observed that the *Roberts* case allows the trial court "discretion" to not allow a "day in the life" video to be shown to a prospective jury. Indeed, the *Roberts* case does not hold that the video must be shown to a jury.

4.6. USING A SUPPLEMENTAL JUROR QUESTIONNAIRE

In Illinois, a written supplemental juror questionnaire is uncommon. However, there is nothing in Supreme Court Rule 234 that prohibits a trial lawyer from drafting and submitting a supplemental questionnaire to the trial judge, which he would like the prospective jurors to answer. It may behoove the skilled trial lawyer to bring a motion in limine for leave to submit such a questionnaire to the entire jury venire when there is a controversial social issue that the facts of the case may trigger once the trial commences but that prospective jurors may be unwilling to publicly discuss. For example, in an auto negligence case involving an intoxicated driver, prospective jurors may be unwilling to openly answer questions about previous arrests or convictions for driving while intoxicated or about treatment and struggles with alcoholism. By submitting a brief written questionnaire for each prospective juror to answer about issues concerning alcohol, the trial lawyer can effectively discover private information from prospective jurors while avoiding the chilling effect from potential embarrassment that a juror would fear. The trial lawyer should present a motion in limine for leave to submit a written supplemental juror questionnaire before jury selection begins, arguing that it is a controversial, potentially embarrassing subject that requires the privacy of a written questionnaire for jurors to answer without fear of embarrassment.

* * *

The motions in limine discussed previously that are effective will help the trial lawyer discover the true attitudes and beliefs of jurors. That knowledge is necessary to intelligently exercise preemptory challenges, which are covered in the next chapter.

RESOURCES ONLINE

TRIAL LAWYERS SHOULD VISIT THE AUTHOR'S WEBSITE AT KURTDLLOYD.COM AND SUBSCRIBE TO HIS BLOG, LLOYD'S TRIAL NOTEBOOK (LLOYDSTRIALNOTEBOOK.COM), TO DOWNLOAD SAMPLE MOTIONS IN LIMINE COVERING THE ISSUES DISCUSSED IN THIS CHAPTER.

CHAPTER 5: PEREMPTORY CHALLENGES TO REMOVE JURORS

A trial lawyer's peremptory challenges are like the killing arrows in his quiver. He gets to shoot any prospective juror for any reason he wants, no questions asked, and remove the juror from his jury. *Black's Law Dictionary* defines the term "peremptory" as: "final; absolute; conclusive; incontrovertible . . . Not requiring any shown cause; arbitrary . . ." The trick or discipline for the skilled trial lawyer is to use his peremptory challenges intelligently and wisely. The skilled trial lawyer also knows that exercising peremptory challenges can often be a strategy in itself. For example, a trial lawyer may exercise a peremptory challenge thereby removing a juror because he knows that the next prospective juror in line to enter the jury box is one his opponent will likely find unfavorable and force a reciprocating peremptory challenge. Of course, this type of strategy is part of the jury deselection process. But this cannot be done if the trial lawyer has not properly conducted a voir dire examination of the prospective jurors and discovered the jurors who likely have negative, biased experiences. The trial lawyer gets to use his peremptory challenge on a prospective juror even though the juror states under oath—no matter how convincingly—that he will keep an open mind, set aside his own beliefs and experiences, and listen to the evidence and apply the law as instructed.

5.1. MINIMUM NUMBER OF PEREMPTORY CHALLENGES SET BY STATUTE

A peremptory challenge is a statutorily created right to excuse a juror for any reason from a jury, despite the juror being completely qualified. In Illinois, the statute provides:

Peremptory Challenges

Each side shall be entitled to 5 peremptory challenges. If there is more than one party on any side, the court may allow each side additional peremptory challenges, not to exceed 3, on account of each additional party on the side having the greatest number of parties. Each side shall be allowed an equal number of peremptory challenges. If the parties on a side are unable to agree upon the allocation of peremptory challenges among themselves, the allocation shall be determined by the court. 735 ILCS 5/2-1106(a).

Each side shall be allowed an equal number of peremptory challenges

A peremptory challenge is the unfettered right to remove a potential juror for any reason. *People v. Dent*, 266 Ill. App.3d 680, 639 N.E.2d 1349, 1352, 203 Ill. Dec. 530 (1st D. 1994). In a one plaintiff and one defendant case, the statute states that each side receives five peremptory challenges. If there is more than one plaintiff or defendant, then the court "may" allow additional peremptory challenges "not to exceed three" for each additional party. 735 ILCS 5/2-116(a); *Curtis v. Lowe*, 338 Ill. App. 463 (2d D. 1949).

5.2. *BATSON* RULE: NO RACIAL BIAS IN EXERCISING PEREMPTORY CHALLENGES

A peremptory challenge should not be used to discriminate against a juror solely because of race. *Batson v. Kentucky*, 476 US 79, 106 S. Ct. 1712 (1986); *People v. Rivera*, 221 Ill. 2d 481 (2006); *People v. Munson*, 206 Ill. 2d 104 (2002); *Mack v. Anderson*, 371 Ill. App.3d 36, 861 N.E.2d 284 (1st D. 2006). For example, in *Mack*, the defendant exercised five peremptory challenges involving black prospective jurors, which was found objectionable by the opposing party. This rule has been extended to include an ethnic affiliation, such as Italian or Native American heritage and exercises of peremptory challenges based solely on gender. *J.E.B. v. Alabama ex rel. T.B.*, 511 US 127, 114 S. Ct. 1419 (1994); *People v. Blackwell*, 164 Ill. 2d 67, 646 N.E.2d 610 (1995). In contrast, the *Batson* rule does not apply to exercises of peremptory challenges based on age. *People v. McGaughy*, 313 Ill. App.3d 656, 730 N.E.2d 127 (3rd D. 2000). In *Lawler v. MacDuff*, 335 Ill. App.3d 144, 151, 153 (2nd D. 2002), the court found that age is not a protected characteristic but that religion is "arguably entitled to some form of heightened scrutiny." The trial court has the authority to sua sponte raise a Batson challenge. *People v. Glasper*, 234 Ill. App.3d 173 (2009).

The effect of *Batson* and its progeny is to limit a party's unfettered right to a peremptory challenge of any juror. As observed in *People v. Dent*: "for 300 years, American jurisprudence considered peremptory challenges in jury cases sacrosanct. A party had the absolute right to use the peremptory challenges allowed them by statute for any reason or no reason at all. Then, in 1986, the United States Supreme Court held that the equal protection clause of our Federal constitution prohibited the prosecution from excluding, by peremptory challenge, prospective jurors 'solely on account of their race.'" Dent, 266 Ill. App.3d 680, 639 N.E.2d 1349, 1352 (1st D. 1994).

The *Batson* rule also applies to criminal and civil jury trials in the state courts of Illinois. *People v. Jackson*, 145 Ill. 2d 43, 582 N.E.2d 125 (1991), judgment vacated on other grounds by *Jackson v. Illinois*, 506 US 802, 113 S. Ct. 32 (1992); *Tucker v. Illinois Power Co.*, 217 Ill. App.3d 748, 577 N.E.2d 919 (5th D. 1991); *Jones v. Rockford Memorial Hospital*, 316 Ill. App.3d 124, 736 N.E.2d 668 (2000). *The Batson* rule applies to both the plaintiff and the defendant. *Haschke v. Uniflow Manufacturing Co.*, 268 Ill. App.3d 1045, 645 N.E.2d 392 (1st D. 1994) (plaintiff's strikes); and *Jones v. Rockford Memorial Hospital*, supra (defendant's strikes). The possible remedies for discriminatory exercise of peremptory challenges are discharging of the entire venire and starting over with a new venire or disallowing the discriminatory challenges and resuming selection with the improperly challenged jurors reinstated in the venire. *Batson*, 106 S. Ct. at 1725, n. 24. However, a sanction such as dismissal of the case because of a single discriminatory challenge is an excessive sanction. *Hunt v. Harrison*, 303 Ill. App.3d 54, 707 N.E.2d 232 (1st D. 1999).

5.2.a. A Party's Burden When Objecting Based on *Batson*

In *Fleming v. Moswin*, 2012 Ill. App (1st) 103475, the court held that "the burden of establishing a prima facie case of purposeful discrimination in jury selection is on the party making the *Batson* claim." *Id.*, at ¶ 41. When addressing a *Batson* challenge, the trial court must follow a methodical three-step approach. *Id.,* at ¶ 35.

First, the moving party must meet his burden of making a prima facie showing that the nonmoving party exercised its peremptory challenge on the basis of race. If a prima facie case is made, the process moves forward.

Second, the burden then shifts to the nonmoving party to articulate a race-neutral explanation for excusing the venireperson. Once the nonmoving party articulates its reasons for excusing the venireperson in question, the process moves forward again.

Third, finally the trial court must determine whether the moving party has carried his burden of establishing purposeful discrimination. At the third step, the trial court evaluates the reasons provided by the nonmoving party as well as claims by the moving party that the proffered reasons are pretextual. *Id.*, ". . . Illinois courts have recognized a general, nonexclusive list of factors relevant to determine whether a prima facie case of discrimination against African-American jurors has been established. These factors include: (1) the racial identity between the moving party and the excluded venireperson; (2) a pattern of strikes against African-American venirepersons; (3) a disproportionate use of peremptory challenges against African-American venirepersons; (4) the level of African-American representation in the venire as compared to the jury; (5) the questions and statements during voir dire examination and while exercising peremptory challenges; (6) whether the excluded African-American venirepersons were a heterogeneous group sharing race as their only common characteristic; and (7) the race of the various parties and the witnesses." *Id.*, at ¶ 47.

Any "ambiguities in the record will be construed against" the party making the *Batson* claim. *Flemming*, at ¶ 48.

* * *

As shown here, there are relatively few restrictions on the use of peremptory challenges against jurors. The skilled lawyer learns the art of challenging biased jurors for any possible cause and saving those precious peremptory challenges for the jurors that he simply believes don't fit the profile of the type of juror he wants. Learning this art comes from experience and reviewing research or conducting it personally, such as by holding focus groups, but it starts with knowing the applicable law. The next chapter goes into detail on all the types of bias that allow challenging jurors for cause.

ONLINE RESOURCES

TRIAL LAWYERS SHOULD VISIT THE AUTHOR'S WEBSITE AT KURTDLLOYD.COM AND SUBSCRIBE TO HIS BLOG, LLOYD'S TRIAL NOTEBOOK (LLOYDSTRIALNOTEBOOK.COM), TO DOWNLOAD A COPY OF "VOIR DIRE WORKBOOK" THAT WILL HELP IN PREPARING A STRATEGY FOR EXERCISING PEREMPTORY CHALLENGES IN THEIR CASE.

CHAPTER 6: CHALLENGES FOR CAUSE

Establishing "cause" to remove a juror may be the most challenging part of voir dire. Too often, the trial lawyer elicits from a prospective juror that he holds a personal bias against his client, but the trial judge denies the attorney's motion to remove the juror for cause because the juror claims that he can set aside his personal bias and be fair to both sides. Of course, a prospective juror who is seated among forty-one other potential jurors almost always is reluctant to readily admit to his fellow jurors that he cannot be fair. The juror doesn't believe, want to believe, or even think that he could have a personal bias that makes him unfair. The juror wants to believe that he can keep an "open mind" about the evidence and the law. Therefore, wanting to believe that he is a "fair" man, when the judge asks him if he can set aside his personal beliefs and be fair to both sides he quickly says yes.

The trial lawyer who is faced with this juror must now ask voir dire questions to the juror and try to prove that the juror is mistaken about his idea of fairness. The trial lawyer must establish that this juror may carry his personal bias into the jury deliberations and that it may interfere with his open-minded fairness, meaning that his life experiences and beliefs may cloud his decision about the case. Voir dire questioning techniques for establishing cause are set forth in chapter 8. What follows in this chapter is the case law defining the standard for proving cause to remove an objectionable juror. Developing a thorough understanding of the necessary proof of cause to remove a biased juror is the foundation that the trial lawyer must know in order to develop the voir dire questioning techniques to prevail.

6.1. THE "OPEN-MINDED" JUROR

In Illinois, a trial lawyer for a party has a statutory right to request removal of a prospective juror who is unfair or biased toward a party, otherwise known as challenging a juror for cause. 735 ILCS 5/2-1105.1 However, except for physical impairment, the statute does not define what constitutes sufficient "cause" for removal. Instead, the trial lawyer must rely on the case law for what constitutes sufficient evidence of "cause."

Whether a potential juror will be fair and impartial in a trial depends on his "state of mind." *People v. Cole*, 54 Ill. 2d 401, 413 (1973). The Illinois Supreme Court in *Cole* has held that a prospective juror who states under oath that he can set aside his personal beliefs, opinions, and associations and keep an "open mind" while listening to the evidence and following the law is qualified to be a juror. *Id.* The juror's impartiality is a state of mind. *Id.* A trial lawyer's mere suspicion of bias in a juror is not evidence of juror bias. The court in *Cole* explicitly overruled the prior line of cases for excusing a juror based on mere suspicion. *Id.* To prove grounds for cause to remove a juror, the lawyer must show through actual evidence that the juror possesses a disqualifying state of mind. *Id.* For example, a juror who states that he holds a fixed or decided opinion that a defendant is either guilty or innocent proves that he does not possess an open state of mind. *Id.*

In *Cole*, the Illinois Supreme Court established the current, prevailing "open-minded" standard for determining whether a juror was qualified to serve on a jury. Studying the *Cole* decision is very illuminating as to what constitutes "cause" to remove a juror. In *Cole*, after the defense had exhausted its peremptory challenges, a new prospective juror stepped into the jury box with the following background:

- He knew the prosecuting state's attorney and the assistant state's attorney. *Id.*, at 411
- He had worked for the state's attorney in his election campaign. *Id.*, 415
- He was a witness for the state in a case in which he was privately employed. *Id.*, 415
- He had spoken to one of the deceased victims a year before the alleged crime. *Id.*

- A witness for the state had a sister married to the prospective juror's son, but he had not spoken to the witness for three to four years. *Id.*, 412
- He was a friend of the sheriff and had spoken to him about things in the news about the alleged murder. *Id.* He had recently served as the treasurer for the sheriff's campaign fund. *Id.*
- A physician testifying as a material witness for the state had been the juror's past neighbor and personal physician. *Id.*

After the trial court's voir dire examination, the defense challenged this prospective juror for cause, which the trial judge denied. *Id.*, at 412. Affirming the denial for cause, the *Cole* court held that the trial judge's determination that a prospective juror possesses the state of mind that will allow him to be fair and impartial during the trial is sufficient to deny a challenge for cause. *Id.*, at 414.

Under *Cole*, the trial judge can rely on the statements of the juror as evidence of his state of mind. *Id.* The prospective juror stated:

- He had no opinion as to the guilt of the defendant.
- He would give the testimony of witnesses with whom he was not acquainted the same weight as those witnesses with whom he was acquainted.
- He "believed he could" disregard anything that he had heard outside the courtroom and base his verdict solely on the evidence.
- "I'm human like everybody else . . . ," but he would not let associations with the State's Attorney's Office interfere with his duties if selected as a juror.
- He would render a fair and impartial verdict if selected. *Id.*, at 412.

The *Cole* court's holding that "the mere suspicion of bias" was insufficient cause to remove a jury overruled any prior Illinois case law to the contrary. *Id.* Absent some evidence of lack of credibility in the juror's statements, the trial judge's determination that the prospective juror statements were truthful shall suffice to defeat a challenge for cause. There is no longer any presumption of bias. *Id.*

Following *Cole*, in both civil and criminal cases, the Illinois appellate courts have found routinely that a trial judge may give great weight to a prospective juror's sworn statement that he can set aside his personal beliefs or opinions that may indicate bias and render a verdict based on the evidence and the law. *People v. Williams*, 161 Ill. 2d 1, 54, 641 N.E.2d 296 (1994); *Lambie v. Schneider*, 305 Ill. App.3d 421, 430 (1999). Without more evidence from the juror, the trial judge's determination that a prospective juror possesses the state of mind that will enable him to be fair and impartial rests in his sound discretion, and his determination should not be set aside unless it is against the manifest weight of the evidence. *Vrzal v. Contract Transportation Systems Co*, 312 Ill. App.3d 755 (1st D. 2000); *Taylor v. R.D. Morgan & Associates, Ltd.*, 205 Ill. App.3d 682 (5th D. 1990).

At common law, the Illinois courts have found very few fact scenarios where prospective jurors are per se biased and should be removed for cause. See, e.g., *Marcin v. Kipfer*, 117 Ill. App.3d 1065, 1067 (4th D. 1983). (A prospective juror's current physician-patient relationship with the defendant created per se bias.) Otherwise, the Illinois appellate courts have held that the trial judge is in a superior position to observe a juror's demeanor, body language, and oral answers and assess the juror's credibility when stating that he will set aside his personal beliefs or opinions and listen to the evidence and follow the law put to him. *Williams*, at 52–54; *Taylor, supra.*

6.2. THE OBJECTIONABLE JUROR EXCUSED FOR CAUSE

The following are cases where a juror was successfully challenged for cause.

6.2.a. Juror Who Has Bias or Prejudice toward a Party Is Cause to Remove

It has long been established that a prospective juror's bias or prejudice, expressed or implied, toward either party, constitutes grounds for challenge for cause and warrants disqualification, whenever such bias would control a juror's judgment or interfere with his duty to act impartially. *People v. Hobbs*, 35 Ill. 2d 263 (1966).

6.2.b. Juror Who Testifies "Cannot Be Objective. No Way" Is Biased

A prospective juror who either has a definite opinion either on the merits of the case or on a determinative fact in the case is biased and subject to removal for cause. *Vrzal v. Contract Transportation Systems Co*, 312 Ill. App.3d 755 (1st D. 2000) citing *People v. Williams*, 173 Ill. 2d 48, 66–67 (1996).

6.2.c. **Juror Who Favors a Party Is Biased and Should Be Removed**

In a civil case for damages under a statute, a prospective juror who testifies that if the evidence were evenly balanced, he would be "inclined" to find for the plaintiff or "lean against the defendant" is incompetent and biased. *Chicago & Alton Railroad Co. v. Adler*, 56 Ill. 344 (1870). To deny a challenge for cause regarding a juror who will not require a preponderance of evidence is error. *Id.* Further, where a juror is inclined toward a party, the trial court's instructions will not correct or cure the bias. *Id.*

6.2.d. **Juror Who Expresses Doubt or Reluctance to Be Impartial Is Cause to Remove**

In a case where two prospective jurors represented to the trial judge that they would listen to the evidence and could be fair, the trial judge was reversed for denial of the defendant's cause motions to remove the jurors, because both jurors also had expressed "doubt" and "reluctance to assume an impartial position" as required of them as jurors. *People v. Stone*, 61 Ill. App.3d 654, 667 (5th D. 1978).

In *People v. Pendleton*, 279 Ill. App.3d 669 (1st D. 1996), a prospective juror who expressed doubt that she could be fair in a case involving a gun because she had been a prior victim of a crime involving a gun should have been excused, despite the best attempts at rehabilitation. (Note: the alleged crime had significant similarity to the juror's personal experience.)

6.2.e. **Juror's Inconsistent Statements toward Following the Law Are Cause to Remove**

In *People v. Pendleton*, 279 Ill. App.3d 669 (1st D. 1996), the court held that a prospective juror who gave inconsistent statements during voir dire should have been excused for cause. Even though the juror said she would follow the law despite a personal belief that the defendant was guilty if it had come as far as trial, the *Pendleton* court found that the totality of her examination indicated an inability to hold the state to its burden of proof beyond a reasonable doubt.

In *People v. Shaw*, 186 Ill. 2d 301, 713 N.E.2d 1161 (1998), the trial judge's removal of a prospective juror for cause based on "contradictory" statements about the death penalty was not held in error. The judge has discretion which will not be doubted. *Id.*

In *People v. Delgado*, 231 Ill. App.3d 117 (1992), the prospective juror had a "close friend" who died from a drug overdose and the defendant on trial was charged in a controlled substance case. When asked if he could be fair and impartial, the juror each time equivocated. The *Delgado* court held it was an error not to excuse the juror for cause.

6.2.f. **Juror's Contradictory Body Language Establishes Challenge for Cause**

In *People v. Harris*, 225 Ill. 2d 1, 33, 866 N.E.2d 162, 181 (2007), despite the prospective juror's statements that he could set aside his personal beliefs and follow the law and listen to the evidence, the juror's body language and demeanor exhibited disagreement with his verbal answers. While saying he could set aside personal beliefs, he repeatedly shook his head in a contradictory "no" manner. The *Harris* court held that the juror's responses were contradictory and ambiguous; therefore, plaintiff's motion for cause was properly granted because ambiguity existed as to whether he was impartial or could fulfill his duties as a juror.

6.2.g. Juror's "Unsure" Equivocal Commitment That She Could Set Aside Personal Beliefs and Follow the Law and the Evidence Is Cause to Remove

A trial judge who refused to excuse a juror for cause when the juror testified that she couldn't say her "background" would not cloud her judgment against a claim, resulted in that jury verdict being reversed in *Thompson v. Altheimer & Gray*, 248 F.3d 621, 627 (7th Cir., 2001). When a prospective juror manifests a prior belief that is both material and contestable (it is not bias to cling to a personal belief that no rational person would question), it is the judge's duty to determine whether the juror is capable of suspending that belief for the duration of the trial. *Id.* When the record contains no assurances that the belief is "shakable," that the prospective juror can exercise a judgment unclouded by that belief, the verdict cannot stand. *Thompson*, 627 citing *United States v. Gonzalez*, 214 F.3d at 1114 (2000) ("When a juror is unable to state that she will serve fairly and impartially, despite being asked repeatedly for such assurances, we can have no confidence that the juror will 'lay aside' her biases or her prejudicial personal experiences and render a fair and impartial verdict." That's this case.) Missing are those "unwavering affirmations of impartiality" that permitted the district judge to find the challenged juror unbiased. *Thompson*, at 653.

6.2.h. Prospective Juror Who "Might" Not Be Fair Because of Prior Experience and Could Not Set Aside Her Prior Experience Is Cause to Remove

In *People v. Harris*, 196 Ill. App.3d 663, 676 (1st D. 1990), although a prospective juror had no preconceived notion against the alleged defendant, she stated that her father had been murdered nine years earlier and that her experience "might" affect her ability to be fair and, when questioned further about setting aside her experience, stated that "it would be tough" and she could not be fair. The *Harris* court held that it was error for the trial court not to excuse the juror for cause. However, the defendant's lawyer, who had exercised a peremptory to remove the juror, waived his objection by not objecting that he was forced to accept a subsequent juror. *Id.*

In *People v. Seaman*, 203 Ill. App.3d 871, 889, 561 N.E.2d 188, 199 (5th D. 1990), a juror who had twice been a victim of a crime and said she "might be prejudiced" because of it and broke down and cried when questioned about it demonstrated possible prejudice. The juror's emotional instability could have prevented her from rationally assimilating the evidence. *Id.*

6.2.i. **Juror's False Statements May Be Cause to Remove**

A juror who misrepresents his background or is dishonest in his answers to voir dire questions may be removed. *People v. Gill*, 240 Ill. App.3d 151, 608 N.E.2d 197, 181 Ill. Dec. 124 (1st D. 1992). In *Gill*, a prospective juror who denied he had ever been accused of a crime, or been a party or witness in a criminal case, was excused for cause because his answers suggested dishonesty.

6.2.j. **Juror Charged with Prior Crimes May Be Cause to Remove**

A person having been charged with various crimes in the past can be sufficient to excuse that person for cause as a potential juror. *People v. Gill*, 240 Ill. App.3d 151, 608 N.E.2d 197, 181 Ill. Dec. 124 (1st D. 1992); *People v. Seaman*, 203 Ill. App.3d 871, 889, 561 N.E.2d 188, 199 (5th D. 1990).

6.2.k. **Juror Who Read or Heard Inflammatory News about Case Immediately Before or During Trial Is Biased**

In *Van Hattem v. Kmart Corp.*, 308 Ill. App.3d 121, 129, 719 N.E.2d 212, 220 (1st D. 1999), the plaintiff was depicted in a television news story about pharmacy errors that was broadcast during the trial and which was the subject of the trial. Despite five jurors stating that they could remain impartial after seeing the broadcast, the *Van Hattem* court reversed the trial court's denial of a mistrial because the palpably prejudicial news broadcast could not be necessarily set aside in the jurors' minds under the circumstances—no matter their oath to be fair. *Id.*, at 129–30.

6.3. THE OBJECTIONABLE JUROR WHO IS REHABILITATED

The impact of the *Cole* decision appears throughout the cases here in which the juror's sworn statement that he can set aside his personal belief, opinion, or experiences was held to remove the potential bias. The juror's promise to keep an open mind rehabilitates him to be an impartial juror.

6.3.a. **Juror's Negative Attitude toward a Legal Defense Is Not Sufficient Grounds**

In *People v. Pasch*, 152 Ill. 2d 133 (1992), the mere fact that three jurors had difficulty believing an insanity defense, including one saying the defense is "overused," does not mean they should be disqualified for cause, because the jurors also testified that they could fairly and impartially hear the evidence.

6.3.b. **Juror's Reading Prior Prejudicial News Story Is Not Cause**

In a personal injury case alleging a pothole defect in a city street, jurors' testimony that they had read or heard recent news reports about the defendant city's failure to maintain streets by filling potholes did not establish cause. Jurors also each testified that they could set aside impressions and listen to the evidence, even though one juror expressed some hesitancy. *Parson v. City of Chicago*, 117 Ill. App.3d 383 (1st D. 1983). Note: the news story was related to events two years after the occurrence at issue in the case.

People v. Gendron, 41 Ill. 2d 351, 355 (1968) held that pretrial publicity about a crime is not grounds to challenge for cause jurors who had read newspaper articles about the alleged crimes but who also denied having any preconceived notions as to the defendant's guilt or innocence. *Id.* See also, *People v. Spagnola*, 123 Ill. App.2d 171 (1st D. 1978).

6.3.c. **Juror's "Uncertainty" about Effect of Prior Personal Experiences Is Not Sufficient Cause**

In *People v. Reid*, 272 Ill. App.3d 301 (1st D. 1995), the defendant was charged with delivery of a controlled substance (cocaine), and a prospective juror was questioned who had many prior experiences involving drugs, including a cocaine-abusing business partner who caused the business to fail and a brother-in-law and sister-in-law abusing cocaine and undergoing drug rehabilitation. When asked if his prior experiences had caused him to have any "preconceived notions" about the case, the juror responded: "I would try not to think it would. I don't know what might happen when the trial starts." Further, the juror also stated that he thought he could keep an open mind and give both sides a fair trial. *Id.*, 303. The *Reid* court affirmed the trial judge's denial of a motion for cause.

In *People v. Martin*, 271 Ill. App.3d 346, 353 (1st D. 1995), when asked if there was any reason why he could not be fair and impartial, the juror answered:

I don't think so.

In follow-up questioning, the same juror more specifically stated:

Like I said, I don't think so. I haven't heard any evidence yet.

The trial judges' refusal to strike the juror for cause was found not to be an abuse of discretion. *Id.*, 353.

6.3.d. **Juror's Commitment to "Try" to Follow the Law Sufficient to Overcome Personal Belief**

In *People v. Johnson*, 162 Ill. App.3d 952 (1st D. 1987), a prospective juror was a gun control advocate, and the defendant was on trial for an alleged armed robbery. The juror stated that she "would try" to be fair and impartial. *Id.*, 954. The *Johnson* court held that the trial judge's decision to deny a motion for cause was not an abuse of discretion. *Id.*

6.3.e. **Juror's Commitment to "Do My Best" Not to Allow Personal Experience to Influence Was Sufficient to Deny Cause**

In *People v. Tipton*, 222 Ill. App.3d 657, 664 (1991), the prospective juror had a sister who had been raped five years earlier and the case on trial involved sexual assault. When asked if her sister's assault would influence her consideration of the case, she stated: "I don't know. I honestly don't know. I would try . . . do my best." The *Tipton* court held that the denial of the motion for cause to remove was not an abuse of discretion.

6.3.f. **Juror's Attitudes in Favor of Tort Reform Is Not Per Se Cause**

A prospective juror who testifies that he favors "tort reform" is not per se biased and, therefore, subject to disqualification for cause. *Vrzal v. Contract Transportation Systems Co*, 312 Ill. App.3d 755 (1st D. 2000). The *Vrzal* court reasoned that no abuse occurred in denying plaintiff's motion for cause, because after repeated questioning of the juror, the juror testified that she could be fair to both sides, could keep an open mind, was "an honest" person, did not have a limit to the amount of damages she could award, and could follow the law even though she did not like it. The *Vrzal* court relied upon *People v. Williams*, 173 Ill. 2d 48, 66–67 (1996), which held that it is not error to deny a motion for cause against a juror who stated that he had bias against guns and their use and who expressed doubts about being unfair, because he later was rehabilitated by also testifying that he "would hear it out" and would decide the case on the law and evidence regardless of bias toward guns.

6.3.g. **Juror's Hesitation about Awarding Damages for Pain and Suffering Based on Frequency and Amount of Liabilities Awarded Is Not Per Se Cause**

In *Flynn v. Edmonds*, 236 Ill. App.3d 770, 780 (4th D. 1992), a prospective juror was asked:

Do you have any problems with the idea that a patient or person involved in an automobile accident is able to come into court and ask for damages not only for medical expenses but also for pain and suffering that might be in excess of the actual medical expenses and loss?

The prospective juror responded:

I wouldn't, I would not have difficulty awarding it if the evidence so said that. I guess my hesitation here is the frequency and the amount of liabilities that this country is going through right now.

The *Flynn* court held that the prospective juror's answers did not constitute per se cause to remove the juror. *Id.*

6.3.h. **Juror's Negative Feelings about People Who Bring Unnecessary Lawsuits Not Per Se Cause**

In *Addis v. Exelon Generation Co.*, 378 Ill. App.3d 781, 792–93 (1st D. 2007), a prospective juror in a wrongful discharge case stated that she had strong, negative feelings about people who bring lawsuits and that too many lawsuits are unnecessary. However, on further questioning, the juror stated that her opinions on lawsuits would not affect her ability to remain impartial and that employees who feel they are justified in bringing a lawsuit have a right to do so. The *Addis* court affirmed the denial of the plaintiff's motion for cause giving great weight to the prospective juror's statement that she could be fair and impartial. *Id.*

6.3.i. **Juror Sympathy toward a Party Is Not Per Se Cause**

In a wrongful death case, the trial judge's denial of a challenge for cause against a prospective juror who testified that she had sympathy for the widow was upheld because she also testified that she could set her sympathy aside and fairly and honestly decide the case and because the judge instructed the jury to put sympathy aside, which cured potential bias. *Romines v. Illinois Motor Freight, Inc.*, 21 Ill. App.2d 380 (2nd D. 1959).

In a personal injury case, although a prospective juror made a statement that he would have sympathy for a "young man who lost his leg" and not the railroad, the juror was not incompetent, because he swore to obey his oath and do justice between the parties. *Chicago & W. I. R. Co v. Bingenheimer*, 116 Ill. 226, 232 (1886).

6.3.j. Prior Claims: Juror Is Not Per Se Biased Because Juror Was Involved in Prior Accident, Claim, or Settlement against the Same Defendant

A prospective juror who testifies to a prior accident involving the defendant, and receiving a settlement to her satisfaction even though she still experiences some pain, is not per se biased or adversarial to the defendant. *Magna Trust Co. v. Illinois Cent. R. Co.*, 313 Ill. App.3d 375, 390 (5th D. 2000). The trial judge's denial for cause was affirmed, particularly because the juror had stated she could be fair and impartial. *Id.*

6.3.k. Juror Who Reads Medical Literature Critical of Malpractice Cases Is Not Per Se Biased

A prospective juror who stated that he reads and is exposed to opinions in medical publications critical of medical malpractice lawsuits does not establish a probable bias in favor of the defendant. *Taylor v. R.D. Morgan & Associates, Ltd*, 205 Ill. App.3d 682 (5th D. 1990). The juror also stated that he did not believe what he read in the publications. *Id.*

6.4. JUROR'S RELATIONSHIP TO A PARTY OR WITNESS MAY CREATE PRESUMED BIAS

In *People v. Cole*, 54 Ill. 2d 401, 413 (1973), the Illinois Supreme Court recognized that there are certain relationships that create presumed bias that disqualifies a person from jury service, such as a prospective juror who is related to a party by blood or sanguinity or who has a direct relationship with a party. The Illinois appellate courts have commented that "the degree of closeness of a prospective juror to party can demonstrate bias." *Lair v. Illinois Central Gulf Railroad* (Ill. C. G. R. Co.), 208 Ill. App.3d 51, 79 (5th D. 2011).

"The trend of authority is to exclude from juries all persons who by reason of their business or social relations, past or present, with either of those parties, could be suspected of possible bias." *Marcin, supra* (4th D. 1983), citing Hunter, *Trial Handbook for Illinois Lawyers*, sec. 15.14 (5th ed. 1983) with approval. The *Marcin* court held that a current physician-patient relationship between the defendant and prospective juror created per se bias. See also, *People v. Green*, 199 Ill. App.3d 927, 930 (1990), where a prospective juror was employed as a secretary in the State's Attorney's Office, which was prosecuting the case against the defendant, and the court held she should have been excused for cause, despite testifying to the ability to be fair and impartial; *People v. Stremmel*, 258 Ill. App.3d 93, 111 (2nd D. 1994), where the court held that a prospective juror who is a police officer employed by the same police department is per se biased, particularly where he would be weighing testimony of civilian witnesses versus police officers, despite his testimony that he could be fair and impartial.

However, despite the *Marcin* case alleging a trend to exclude jurors based on a social or business relationship, the *Marcin, Green,* and *Stremmel* cases are the only cases since *Cole* finding a presumption of bias.

6.5. MALPRACTICE CASES: JUROR'S RELATIONSHIP TO DEFENDANT PHYSICIAN

In Illinois, many cases involving medical malpractice have examined the question of juror bias against the plaintiff based on some type of juror relationship or connection to a defendant physician.

6.5.a. **Juror Who Has Current Patient-Physician Relationship with a Party Is Per Se Biased and Should Be Removed for Cause**

A juror who has a current patient-physician relationship with the physician on trial establishes a per se bias that is a challenge for cause. *Marcin v. Kipfer*, 117 Ill. App.3d 1065, 1067 (4th D. 1983). The defense verdict was reversed for the trial judge's failure to excuse two jurors who were current patients of the defendant. The judge was reversed even though the prospective jurors each testified that their relationship would not make it difficult to serve and treat the defendant the same as any other defendant. *Id.*

However, if the evidence from a prospective juror involves something a step removed from a current patient-physician relationship (see following examples), the courts have not found a presumption of bias. *Roach v. City of Springfield*, 157 Ill. 2d 29, 47 (1993); *Lambie v. Schneider*, 305 Ill. App.3d 421, 430 (4th D. 1999).

6.5.b. **Juror Being Former Patient of Defendant Ob-Gyn Strongly Suggests Per Se Bias**

In *Fleeman v. Fischer*, 244 Ill. App.3d 753, 755 (5th D. 1993), commenting that a strong argument for removal for cause existed, the court observed that a prospective juror having been delivered successfully by the defendant was such a "significant event," although in the past, that the relationship was too close for her to be objective. However, the *Fleeman* court found that the plaintiff had waived the argument for a challenge for cause by not exhausting his preemptory challenges on such jurors. *Id.*

6.5.c. **Juror Whose Spouse Has Current Patient-Physician Relationship Is Not Per Se Biased**

A juror's spouse being a current patient of the defendant does not establish per se bias.

Roach v. City of Springfield, 157 Ill. 2d 29, 47 (1993), reversed on other grounds. Distinguishing *Marcin* on its facts, the Roach court noted that closeness of the spouse's relationship to the defendant must be assessed on a case-by-case basis. Importantly, in *Roach*, the court noted that the juror had testified post-trial that he did not even know of his wife's patient relationship with the defendant until halfway through the trial and did not think it "significant" to report; therefore, no prejudice was shown.

6.5.d. **Juror Whose Son Was Prior Patient of Defendant Is Not Per Se Biased**

A prospective juror who had a son treated by the defendant seven or eight years earlier was not per se biased. *Flynn v. Edmonds*, 236 Ill. App.3d 770, 780 (4th D. 1992). In *Flynn*, distinguishing *Marcin* on its facts, the court noted that the juror said his son's prior treatment would not give the defendant physician an advantage and he would not hesitate in returning a verdict for the plaintiff. *Id.*

6.5.e. **Juror Employed in the Medical Field Is Not Per Se Biased**

A juror's employment in the medical field, his marriage to a nurse, and his acquaintance with the defendant's witnesses does not establish a probable bias in favor of the defendant for which the judge should have granted a cause motion. *Taylor v. R.D. Morgan & Associates, Ltd*, 205 Ill. App.3d 682 (5th D. 1990). Again, the juror stated he could be fair. *Id.*

6.5.f. **Juror Who Has In-Law Who Is Defendant's Patient Is Not Per Se Biased**

A prospective juror whose father-in-law underwent open-heart surgery by the defendant and because his condition was declining would probably see the defendant physician again was not per se biased. *Lambie v. Schneider*, 305 Ill. App.3d 421, 430 (4th D. 1999).

6.6. RELATIONSHIP TO A PARTY'S EMPLOYER

6.6.a. Juror with the Same Employer May Constitute Per Se Bias

A prospective juror who is a police officer employed by the same police department that investigated a crime is per se biased, particularly where he would be weighing testimony of civilian witnesses versus police officers, despite his testimony that he could be fair and impartial. *People v. Stremmel*, 258 Ill. App.3d 93, 111 (2nd D. 1994).

Similarly, in *People v. Green*, 199 Ill. App.3d 927, 930 (1990), the court held that a secretary who was employed in the State's Attorney's Office, which was prosecuting the case, should have been excused for cause despite testifying to the ability to be fair and impartial.

However, a prospective juror working for the same large employer as a party in the case at best raises a mere suspicion of bias but is not per se evidence of bias. *Grady v. Marchini*, 375 Ill. App.3d 174 (4th D. 2007).

6.6.b. Juror with Family Members Employed by Defendant Affiliate Insufficient Cause

A juror who testified that she had an aunt and nephew who were employed by ComEd, an affiliate of the defendant but did not know what jobs that they held, did not establish prejudice. *Addis v. Exelon Generation Co.*, 378 Ill. App.3d 781, 792 (1st D. 2007). Again, the juror testified that she could put family ties aside and be fair and impartial. *Id.*

6.7. OTHER INDIRECT JUROR RELATIONSHIPS

6.7.a. Family Relationship Shared by Juror and Plaintiff

A prospective juror having a child related to a child of the plaintiff does not establish bias. *Grady v. Marchini*, 375 Ill. App.3d 174 (4th D. 2007). The *Grady* court considered the question of the potential bias of a juror with a child who was related to a child of the plaintiff, and both children having played softball together ten years ago. But because the juror also stated that she could be fair and impartial, the court held the relationship to be not objectionable for cause.

6.7.b. **Juror Relationship to Insurance Companies**

A prospective juror who is an insured of a defendant mutual insurance company is biased. *Rains v. Schutte*, 53 Ill. App.2d 217 (5th D. 1964).

6.7.c. **Juror Who Is Friend of State's Attorney Not Biased**

People v. Kuntu, 196 Ill. 2d 105 (2001).

6.7.d. **Juror Who Has Father Who Was Represented by Attorney for a Party Not Biased**

Laird v. Ill. C. G. RR, 208 Ill. 3d 51, 78 (5th D. 1991).

6.7.e. **Juror Who Simply Knows a Witness Is Not Biased**

People v. Cesarz, 44 Ill. 2d 180 (1969).

6.7.f. **Juror Who Has Been a Party to a Lawsuit Is Not Per Se Biased**

Because a prospective juror has been "sued" or "sued someone" does not, without more, establish sufficient grounds for cause, even if the juror did not reveal it before being selected. *Davis v. International Harvester Co.*, 167 Ill. App.3d 814, 521 N.E.2d 1282 (2nd D. 1988).

6.8. PERFECTING OBJECTIONS TO JURORS

The trial lawyer, when making a challenge for cause, must specifically state the grounds, including why the juror is biased, which are supported by facts. *Fandich v. Allstate Insurance Co.*, Inc., 25 Ill. App.3d 301, 307–308 (1st D. 1974); *People v. Cole*, 54 Ill. 2d 401, 414 (1973). However, when the trial judge does not sua sponte remove a juror for cause, the trial lawyer who believes a juror should be excused for cause must request it. The failure to make such a request constitutes a waiver of the claim that the juror should have been excused for cause. *Fleeman v. Fischer*, 244 Ill. App.3d 753, 613 N.E.2d 836, 184 Ill. Dec. 519 (5th D. 1993).

The trial plaintiff's lawyer has the burden of showing that the juror possesses a disqualifying state of mind, i.e. bias, prejudice, fixed opinion, when challenging a juror for cause. *People v. Cole*, 54 Ill. 2d 401, 413. A lawyer's "mere suspicion" of a juror's bias or impartiality is not evidence and does not disqualify a juror for cause. *People v. Kuntu*, 196 Ill. 2d 105 (2001); *Grady v. Marchini*, 375 Ill. App.3d 174 (4th D. 2007).

Any objections made during jury selection, including challenges for cause, must be raised within the party's post-trial motion; otherwise, the issue is waived on appeal. *Brown v. Decatur Memorial Hospital*, 83 Ill. 2d 344 (1980).

Where a party desires to have the appellate court review the propriety of a question asked on voir dire, the precise questions must be included in the record on appeal. Otherwise, that appellate court would be required to guess or conjecture as to the phraseology and content thereof, which it will not do. *People v. Chamness*, 129 Ill. App.3d 871 (1st D. 1984).

6.9. PRESERVING ERROR FOR DENIAL OF CHALLENGE FOR CAUSE

To preserve for appeal an error in a motion for challenge for cause of a juror, the lawyer must have already exhausted his preemptory challenges, so that the result was that an objectionable juror was forced upon him. *Roach v. City of Springfield*, 157 Ill. 2d 29, 47 (1993); *Grady v. Marchini*, 375 Ill. App.3d 174 (4th D. 2007). The party claiming that an objectionable juror was foisted upon him must also show prejudice regarding any new, objectionable juror, after he has exhausted his peremptory challenges. *People v. Reid*, 272 Ill. App.3d 301 (1st D. 1995).

* * *

In challenging a prospective juror for cause, the Illinois courts give great weight to a juror's statement that he can set aside his experiences and current or past relationship to a party and be fair. In part, this reflects the reality of Illinois demographics. Outside of the Chicago metropolitan area, rural counties have a limited, more interconnected jury pool. It may be hard to find anyone who doesn't have some kind of relationship or experiences with the only doctor in town or a major local employer. So the courts give the small town juror's statement that he can be fair preference over any potential bias. And while those cases are set forth in the precedents covered in this chapter, the reality is that in Chicago, with its much larger and more diverse pool of jurors, the court is more likely to grant a trial lawyer a challenge for cause against a prospective juror.

The trial lawyer must be able to rely on the truthfulness of the juror's answers in order to make an intelligent challenge. When it turns out the juror has misrepresented his background, opinion, or actions, the trial lawyer can begin or renew a challenge for cause to remove that juror, a process covered in the next chapter.

ONLINE RESOURCES

TRIAL LAWYERS SHOULD VISIT THE AUTHOR'S WEBSITE AT KURTDLLOYD.COM AND SUBSCRIBE TO HIS BLOG, LLOYD'S TRIAL NOTEBOOK (LLOYDSTRIALNOTEBOOK.COM), TO DOWNLOAD A COPY OF "VOIR DIRE WORKBOOK" THAT WILL HELP IN DRAFTING AND ORGANIZING AN EFFECTIVE SET OF VOIR DIRE SUBJECT QUESTIONS DESIGNED TO ELICIT OR ESTABLISH JUROR BIAS AND ESTABLISH A CHALLENGE FOR CAUSE IN THEIR CASE.

CHAPTER 7: JUROR MISREPRESENTATION OR MISCONDUCT

In the age of the Internet, reports of jurors violating their sworn oath and "googling" or searching for independent information about the case, the parties, the attorneys, or a contested issue has become ubiquitous.[1] In jury trials, people's lives and livelihoods are at stake. A trial lawyer cannot effectively present a case to a jury when, unbeknownst to him, a juror has "spiked" the case with extraneous information, which probably is either irrelevant or prejudicial. For example, in *McGee v. City of Chicago*, 365 Ill. Dec. 866 (1st D. 2012), during the trial, a juror independently searched on the Internet for published articles on the subject of the plaintiff's alleged memory lapses, which impacted witness credibility and brought that information into the jury room, resulting in a new trial.

Similarly, across the country, trial lawyers are searching the Internet for the background of a selected juror and comparing it to the juror's sworn answers during voir dire, then discovering that a selected juror has either lied or withheld background information, e.g. litigation history, from the parties during voir dire.[2] In *Strawder v. City of Chicago*, 294 Ill. App.3d 399 (1st D. 1998), the trial judge was reversed on appeal for failure to remove a

1 | Diane Wiley, "Jurors Googling & Blogging—Can a Juror Pledge Stop Them?" *The Jury Expert*, 27(4), 2015.

2 | John G. Browning, "As Voir Dire Becomes Voir Google, Where Are the Ethical Lines Drawn," *The Jury Expert*, 25(3), 2013.

juror who had answered falsely during voir dire about her background. In this chapter, the law is set forth for removing a juror for misconduct or newly discovered bias that the juror failed to disclose during selection. *Thornton v. Garcini*, 364 Ill. App.3d 612, 618 (3rd D. 2006). Hopefully, the principles here will prevent a "rogue" juror from hijacking the jury trial process.

7.1. JUROR BIAS DISCOVERED AFTER JUROR SELECTED

A juror may be discharged after being selected and sworn, upon a showing of good cause, and a new trial is not warranted unless the opposing party proves prejudice. *Pekelder v. Edgewater Automotive Co.*, 68 Ill. 2d 136, 139, 368 N.E.2d at 901 (1977); *Barton v. Chicago & Northwestern Transp.*, 325 Ill. App.3d 1005, 757 N.E.2d 533 (2001); *Addis v. Exelon Generation Co.*, 378 Ill. App.3d 781, 792 (1st D. 2007). The trial judge's decision to discharge a juror during trial is within his sound discretion. *Lowe v. Norfolk & Western Ry. Co.*, 124 Ill. App.3d 80, 105, 463 N.E.2d 792 (1984).

7.1.a. **False Answers Are Cause to Remove**

In *Strawder v. City of Chicago*, 294 Ill. App.3d 399 (1st D. 1998), the appellate court stated that when new information is revealed that tends to contradict a sworn juror's answers, the trial court should allow further inquiry even though voir dire has ended and the trial has commenced. The failure to do so can result in reversible error. In *Strawder*, it was error for the trial court to deny a motion to excuse a juror from the panel who had explicitly made false statements that were material during voir dire.

7.1.b. **Humorous Political Statement Is Not Cause to Remove**

In *Addis v. Exelon Generation Co.*, 378 Ill. App.3d 781, 792 (1st D. 2007), during a trial alleging retaliatory discharge of an employee against a nuclear power company, a sworn juror wore a black T-shirt one day displaying a stick figure in a darkened room peering through a doorway full of light with the caption, "If it weren't for electricity, where would you be?" In chambers, the juror testified that he felt it was humorous but the T-shirt did not reflect either side in his opinion. The *Addis* court affirmed the trial judge's denial of plaintiff's motion for cause. *Id.*

7.1.c. **Juror's Relationship to Witness Is Not Cause to Remove**

In *People v. Campbell,* 126 Ill. App.3d 1028, 1044 (2nd D. 1984), after the third day of trial, a juror learned that the defendant's mother was a witness and her husband worked for the juror's husband, and the juror stated in chambers that she would be "influenced" by the relationship. *Id.*, 1041. The juror had not been told during voir dire that the defendant's mother would be a witness, and she had been "shocked" when the defendant's mother took the stand. *Id.* The *Campbell* court found that although the juror testified that she would be influenced by the relationship, the defendant failed to make a showing how the juror had been influenced. The juror evidence was ambiguous and, therefore, insufficient. The defendant never developed any "actual evidence" of bias or prejudice. *Campbell,* 126 Ill. App.3d at 1044.

7.1.d. **Juror's Unexplored Relationship to Defendant Institution Not Cause to Remove**

In *Harris Trust & Savings Bank v. Abraham-Zwirn,* 314 Ill. App.3d 527 (1st D. 2000), the plaintiff's lawyer asked a prospective juror, who was an in-house defense lawyer, whether anyone in her family had any relationship with the defendant Loyola Hospital, its related medical school, the neonatal intensive care unit, or anything like that, and the juror responded no. The juror was later accepted. The next day, the plaintiff's lawyer discovered that the juror had attended Loyola University and its law school. The *Harris* court held that the plaintiff lawyer's motion for cause to remove the juror was properly denied because the attorney failed to ask the right questions during voir dire. *Id.* The juror had not affirmatively misrepresented her relationship to a party, because she was never specifically asked and did not have to affirmatively volunteer non-responsive information.

7.2. PREJUDICIAL EVENTS IN FRONT OF THE JURY CREATED CAUSE

During trial and after the jury had been sworn, the defendant physician went to the aid of a juror who became unconscious in the jury box. The plaintiff lawyer moved for a mistrial, which was denied. Despite the jurors' statements that they could continue to be fair and impartial and that they were not prejudiced, the Supreme Court held that the unusual event cast the defendant in a favorable light and likely "pre-disposed the jury in Defendant's favor." *Campbell v. Fox*, 113 Ill. 2d 354, 359 (1986).

7.3. JUROR MISCONDUCT

In Illinois, the trial judge instructs the jury about its duties and responsibilities shortly after being sworn. The Illinois Pattern Instructions No. 1.01 devotes considerable time cautioning jurors to not do research or investigation outside of the courtroom, in an attempt to prevent potential juror misconduct. The instruction reads, in part, as follows:

> *[6] You should not do any independent investigation or research on any subject relating to the case. What you may have seen or heard outside the courtroom is not evidence. This includes any press, radio, or television programs and it also includes any information available on the Internet. Such programs, reports, and information are not evidence and your verdict must not be influenced in any way by such material.*
>
> *[7] For example, you must not use the Internet, [including Google,] [Wikipedia,] [[(insert current examples)]], or any other sources that you might use every day, to search for any information about the case, or the law which applies to the case, or the people involved in the case, including the parties, witnesses, lawyers, and judge.*

[8] During the course of the trial, do not discuss this case with anyone--not even your own families or friends, and also not even among yourselves--until at the end of the trial when you have retired to the jury room to deliberate on your verdict. Even though this is hard to do, it will be a violation of these instructions and your oath if you discuss the case with anyone else. [9] You must not provide any information about the case to anyone by any means at all, and this includes posting information about the case, or your thoughts about it, on any device or Internet site, including [blogs,] [chat-rooms,] or [[(insert current examples)]], or any social networking websites, such as [Twitter], [Facebook] or [[(insert current examples)]], or any other means.

[10] You cannot use any electronic devices or services to communicate about this case, Section 1, Page 3 of 17 and this includes [cell-phones,] [smart-phones,] [lap-tops,] [the Internet,] [[(insert current examples)]] and any other tools of technology. The use of any such devices or services in connection with your duties is prohibited.

[11] The reason for these instructions is that your verdict must be based only on the evidence presented in this courtroom and the law I [will provide] [have provided] to you in my instructions. It would be unfair to the parties and a violation of your oath to base your decision on information from outside this courtroom. You should feel free to remind each other that your verdict is to be based only on the evidence admitted in court and that you cannot use information from any other sources. If you become aware of any violation of these instructions, it is your legal duty to report this to me immediately.

[12] Disobeying these instructions could cause a mistrial, meaning all of our efforts have been wasted and we would have to start over again with a new trial. If you violate these instructions, you could be found in contempt of court. Illinois Pattern Jury Instruction 1.01.

7.3.a. **Jurors Performing Their Own Research**

In general, Illinois courts have found that jurors consulting outside, substantive matters was sufficiently prejudicial to warrant a new trial only if those matters were not previously introduced into evidence or if they were not matters within the common experience of laypersons. For example, in *Frede v. Downs*, 101 Ill. App.3d 812 (1st D. 1981), during jury deliberations in a boating accident trial, one of the jurors brought into the jury room a book titled *Piloting, Seamanship and Small Boat Handling*. The trial court limited its inquiry to the use of the book rather than considering its effect, if any, upon the decision-making process of the jurors. However, the appellate court found that the plaintiff had made the requisite showing of probability of prejudice, in light of the fact that the jury read from the book about the rules and duties of skippers and that those duties were specifically at issue in the trial. *Frede*, 101 Ill. App.3d at 813–814.

Haight v. Aldridge Electric Co., 215 Ill. App.3d 353 (2d D. 1991), is another case concerning the jury independently consulting information not in evidence. The *Haight* case involved a truck-car collision at an intersection that occurred at 8:30 p.m. At trial, several witnesses testified concerning the conditions of visibility at the time of the collision. During deliberations, one of the jurors informed the others that he had looked at an almanac that reported that the sunset occurred at around 6 p.m. on the day of the collision. The *Haight* court held that the juror's consultation of the almanac was directly related to a crucial issue in the case—visibility—and that upon its showing, the burden shifted to the prevailing party in the lower court to demonstrate that no prejudice resulted. The *Haight* court found that the burden was not met by the prevailing party and reasoned that while conflicting evidence was presented at trial regarding the visibility conditions at the time of the collision, none of the parties presented evidence as to the time of sunset that evening. Therefore, the court ordered a new trial after concluding that the almanac constituted new evidence that related directly to a crucial issue with which the plaintiff had neither been confronted at trial nor had the opportunity to refute. *Haight*, 215 Ill. App.3d at 369–370.

In *McGee v. City of Chicago*, 365 Ill. Dec. 866 (1st D. 2012), the trial court's failure to question in voir dire a sworn juror regarding research performed outside the courtroom was held an abuse of discretion and grounds for a new trial. See also, *Macias v. Cincinnati Forte,* 277 Ill. App.3d 947, 950–52 (1st D. 1996) (conducting independent research); *Birch v. Drummer,* 139 Ill. App.3d 397, 408–10 (4th D. 1985) (personal investigation of the facts).

7.3.b. **Jurors Exposed to Publicity or News Reports**

In a wrongful death case alleging a defendant pharmacy had mistakenly filled a prescription, five jurors had watched a Channel 5 News television story, "Prescription for Trouble?" which had been broadcast during the trial and included the plaintiff's widow. *Van Hattem v. Kmart Corp*, 308 Ill. App.3d 121 (1st D. 1999). The *Van Hattem* court held the juror conduct was grounds for mistrial based on presumed juror prejudice. Importantly, reversing the trial judge's denial of a mistrial as abuse of discretion, the *Van Hattem* court held that the jurors' responses that they could be fair were insufficient to rehabilitate or restore fairness, observing that "it has been held that jurors themselves are incapable of knowing the effect which prejudicial matters may have upon their unconscious minds." *Van Hattem*, 308 Ill. App.3d 129, citing *People v. Hryciuk*, 5 Ill. 2d 176, 183–84 (1954). Jurors' nods of the head that they could be fair is inadequate evidence of impartiality. The trial judge should have extensively questioned jurors who not only saw the broadcast but also may have heard about the broadcast. *Id.*

A statement of a juror that reading a prejudicial newspaper article has not influenced him should not be considered conclusive. *People v. Hryciuk*, 5 Ill. 2d at 183–84. Instead, the judge should determine by inference whether prejudice has occurred by the character and nature of the prejudicial statements. *Id.*

7.3.c. **Other Juror Misbehavior**

In *Lowe v. Norfolk & Western Ry. Co.*, 124 Ill. App.3d 80, 105, 463 N.E.2d 792 (1984), a sworn juror was annoying another juror by speaking to him during the trial and hitting other jurors and "making expressions toward them." The trial judge's discharge of the juror was found proper.

Other instances of juror misbehavior resulting in being discharged have included:

Intoxication. *Landstrom v. Williamson*, 164 Ill. App.3d 1087, 1089 (4th D. 1987);

Failure to Appear. 705 ILCS 305/15;

Inattention to the Trial. *People v. Gonzalez*, 388 Ill. App.3d 566, 578–79 (1st D. 2008);

Communicating with the Parties or Attorneys. *Jeanery v. Chicago & Interurban Traction*, 306 Ill. 392, 398 (1923).

* * *

Juror misconduct involving researching or reading about cases online is becoming more prevalent as Internet access grows more convenient and pervasive on smartphones. Juror misconduct issues are more frequently arising after the trial starts. For a trial lawyer who has lost a case, it pays to call jurors post-trial, and if they will take the call, to ask if somebody in the jury room was doing something wrong, such as talking about information that wasn't part of the case.

Of course, the most effective time to ask jurors questions is not after a case is lost but before the jury is impaneled. The next chapter explores how to get jurors talking about themselves and their beliefs as much as possible by asking questions that are more apt to produce a truthful answer than just a socially acceptable reply.

ONLINE RESOURCES

TRIAL LAWYERS SHOULD VISIT THE AUTHOR'S WEBSITE AT KURTDLLOYD.COM AND SUBSCRIBE TO HIS BLOG, LLOYD'S TRIAL NOTEBOOK (LLOYDSTRIALNOTEBOOK.COM), TO DOWNLOAD A COPY OF A SAMPLE MOTION RELATING TO JUROR MISCONDUCT.

CHAPTER 8: FRAMING ATTORNEY VOIR DIRE QUESTIONS TO REVEAL JUROR BIAS

How trial lawyers ask voir dire questions matters. Words matter. The choice of word phrasing matters. Prospective jurors respond more openly to a lawyer's voir dire question based on how the question was phrased and structured. For example, does the lawyer ask a question using the more defensiveness-provoking "are you able to" or the more neutral, thought-provoking "might you have some trouble or difficulty" putting aside your personal beliefs about giving money for pain and suffering damages? If a lawyer's questions do not make a prospective juror feel comfortable talking about sharing their beliefs and potential bias, then he will never discover or identify who should be peremptorily excused or challenged for cause.

Jurors rely upon their habits, attitudes, personal experiences, and beliefs to make decisions. Each juror has a lens through which evidence shall be viewed and interpreted. This is their worldview. Jurors deliberate based on their perception of the facts and their own belief systems about the law and arguments.[3] A trial lawyer should try to remember

3 | Matthew L. Ferrara, "The Psychology of Voir Dire," *The Jury Expert*, 22(2), 35-47, 2010.

that each juror, if selected, will look at the case presented and not believe what he sees but rather see what he believes. Jury consultant Richard Gabriel describes this as "confirmation bias." The jurors look to confirm what they already believe.[4]

The trial lawyer's challenge is to ask questions that encourage the juror to answer honestly as opposed to becoming guarded. The lawyer wants to avoid voir dire questioning of a juror that leads to prehabilitation[5] answers. Most jurors suffer from the desire to be socially accepted, like a "good American" or a "good citizen." When asking voir dire questions, the trial lawyer does not want to send a message to the juror that "yes" is the only acceptable answer. Specifically, to discover a prospective juror's beliefs about the issues the trial lawyer (or judge) wants to avoid questions which imply to the juror: I better say "yes" if I want to look good to the court, appear competent to the fellow jurors, and confirm to myself that I am fair-minded. For example, few jurors if asked "are you able to be fair" will answer "no." Prospective jurors either know they cannot be fair but will not admit it or don't know if they can be fair but still answer "yes"—wanting to believe they are fair or to avoid any embarrassment.

In this chapter, suggestions are made about how to frame questions to elicit more honest juror answers instead of shutting the juror off.

Most jurors will not admit that they are not able to do something.

8.1. QUESTIONS THAT PROVOKE DEFENSIVENESS

For example:

> Are you able to set aside your beliefs and listen to the law and the evidence?

Most jurors will not admit that they are not able to do something.

4 | Richard Gabriel, *Acquittal: Secrets of a High-Profile Trial Consultant* (Berkley: 2015), 26.

5 | Jury consultant Hamilton has coined the term "prehabilitation," a term meaning judge or attorney questioning that leads—in fact, often pushes—a prospective juror toward "yes, I can be fair" before the juror's potential bias is revealed or explored. Hamilton, "The Ubiquitous Practice of 'Prehabilitation' Leads Prospective Jurors to Conceal Their Biases," *The Jury Expert*, 26(3), 48-65 , 2014.

> Do you have a problem setting aside your personal experience and listening to the evidence and applying the law?

Again, most jurors do not wish to admit that they have a "problem" or cannot be fair. In each of these examples, the trial lawyer has framed the question using words that do not encourage a prospective juror to divulge his or her beliefs or experiences.

8.2. QUESTIONS THAT ARE NEUTRAL OR THOUGHT PROVOKING

For example:

> If you had to say that you lean one way or the other about deciding that a physician was negligent based on the evidence and law, which way would you lean?
>
> Or,
>
> Some people believe that physicians can make mistakes without being negligent, and other people believe that physicians can be negligent for their mistakes. How do you feel about this?

Each question as worded and framed does not telegraph a right or wrong answer to the juror. Similarly, research has found that honest juror answers go up significantly with this kind of question wording:

> If you were to serve on this jury and you had to decide whether the defendant Dr. Smith was negligent, then:
>
> > "might you have some difficulty" setting aside your beliefs or experiences toward physicians and health care?
>
> Or,

> "might you have some trouble (or "would you struggle") setting aside your attitude toward or experiences with physicians and health care?"

If the prospective juror admits to some potential bias, then the lawyer should simply ask "why?" This allows the juror to answer without the fear of judgment or being wrong. If the lawyer, instead, too quickly then turns to a leading question format, then the risk is that the juror will snap back to the good citizen "yes, I can be fair." More important, the lawyer never discovers or exposes the juror's true beliefs so that, if the juror is negatively biased, the juror can be challenged for cause.

8.3. QUESTIONS THAT PROVE A CHALLENGE FOR CAUSE

In voir dire questioning, the trial lawyer hopes to help prospective jurors reveal their honest beliefs and attitudes toward the case or the issues. At this point, based on the juror's answers, the trial lawyer may decide that a juror is likely biased against his case and must now prove that the juror should be removed for cause. The trial lawyer establishing a proof of a challenge for cause also saves the lawyer from exercising a precious peremptory challenge. The trial lawyer's goal is to establish that, although the prospective juror was rehabilitated by the opposing party by stating that he could set aside his personal experiences and beliefs and be fair, some discrepancies, equivocation, doubt, etc. remain in the answers given, requiring the juror's removal.

As discussed earlier in this chapter, the trial lawyer should ask a prospective juror enough open-ended, nonthreatening questions to get the juror to reveal his true beliefs and experiences. If at some point the lawyer decides the juror is objectionable to the client's case, then it is time to establish cause to remove the juror.

For example, suppose that a prospective juror has answered, "I believe that a doctor is only human, he's doing his best, and I don't know that I could find him negligent." This sentiment is likely the juror's long held belief and is not going to change. If the opposing lawyer is allowed to rehabilitate the juror, that lawyer may very well lead the juror into saying that he could "set aside his belief about doctors," the result of which is to set up a denial for cause. Thus, the questioning lawyer must shift to a line of leading questions that locks the juror into a biased position, which cannot be rehabilitated. For example:

> **Q:** I'm glad that you told us how you feel about doctors. You probably have held this belief for a long time, is that correct?
>
> **A:** Yes. I think so.
>
> **Q:** Can I assume that you're likely to continue to have that belief tomorrow or next week?
>
> **A:** Yes.
>
> **Q:** There wouldn't be anything that would suddenly change your mind?
>
> **A:** No.
>
> **Q:** On a scale of 1 to 10, would you say that the strength of your belief is more than a 5?
>
> **A:** I think so.
>
> **Q:** So I assume that you know your mind and what you believe and you're not going to have someone come along and tell you to set aside your belief?
>
> **A:** Right. Probably true.
>
> **Q:** It's okay to have your belief about doctors. I'm glad you shared it with us. We're each entitled to have our beliefs. So is it safe to say even the judge would not be able to tell you to ignore your beliefs, true?
>
> **A:** True.

After this line of questions and answers, any change in a statement would be contradictory or at least equivocal to any rehabilitation testimony from the juror and solid grounds for cause.

* * *

This chapter has provided some suggestions for wording questions likely to elicit the honest answers necessary to uncover juror bias. It's up to the trial lawyer to learn—or use this manual to look up—the case law to determine the best strategy to use challenges to effectively deselect jurors who are biased. A trial lawyer who doesn't know how to properly pick a jury that can be fair is going to lose his case before it starts.

ONLINE RESOURCES

TRIAL LAWYERS SHOULD VISIT THE AUTHOR'S WEBSITE AT KURTDLLOYD.COM AND SUBSCRIBE TO HIS BLOG, LLOYD'S TRIAL NOTEBOOK (LLOYDSTRIALNOTEBOOK.COM), TO DOWNLOAD A COPY OF "VOIR DIRE WORKBOOK" THAT WILL HELP IN DRAFTING AND ORGANIZING AN EFFECTIVE SET OF VOIR DIRE QUESTIONS FOR THEIR CASE.

CONCLUSION

There's a vast difference between knowing the basics covered in this book and having the experience to be able to apply it in a case as complicated as a medical malpractice case. The complications include not just the medical and scientific aspects but also the benefit of the doubt that juries give doctors and the specific types of questions therefore required for effective jury selection. The smart trial lawyer recognizes when he is in over his head and dealing with something new that is best done with an expert counsel by his side.

The author is available to partner or consult with lawyers who need more help with their cases. The first step is to visit the author's website, KurtDLloyd.com, or his blog, Lloyd's Trial Notebook (LloydsTrialNotebook.com), which have sample questions for voir dire and various motions in limine to file before voir dire starts. That may be enough help for simple negligence cases that a lawyer might get as a result of a traffic mishap. When it comes to the more sophisticated, complicated cases, such as medical malpractice, jury selection becomes even more important and requires a great deal of skill, preparation, and understanding of what a trial lawyer can and cannot ask.

APPENDIX

STATUTES, COURT RULES, AND JURY INSTRUCTIONS APPLICABLE TO JURY SELECTION

705 ILCS 305/2

Statutory Juror Qualification

At the September meeting of the county board in each year in the respective counties in this State, except those that have jury commissioners, the board shall select from the list the number of persons as the judges of the circuit courts, to be held in the county during the succeeding year, may by joint action determine to serve as petit jurors. In counties having jury commissioners, the persons to serve as petit jurors shall be selected by the jury commissioners, as provided by law. County boards, a jury administrator, and jury commissioners may utilize the services of the Administrative Office of the Illinois Courts in making these selections.

Jurors in all counties in Illinois must have the legal qualifications herein prescribed. Jurors must be:

(1) Inhabitants of the county.

(2) Of the age of 18 years or upwards.

(3) Free from all legal exception, of fair character, of approved integrity, of sound judgment, well informed, and able to understand the English language, whether in spoken or written form or interpreted into sign language.

(4) Citizens of the United States of America.

705 ILCS 305/14

Statutory Juror Disqualification

It shall be sufficient cause of challenge of a petit juror that he lacks any one of the qualifications mentioned in Section 2 of this Act;

Or if he is not one of the regular panel, that he has served as a juror on the trial of a cause in any court in the county within one year previous to the time of his being offered as a juror; or that he is a party to a suit pending for trial in that court. It shall be the duty of the court to discharge from the panel all jurors who do not possess the qualifications provided in this Act, as soon as the fact is discovered.

If a person has served on a jury in a court within one year, he shall be exempt from again serving during such year, unless he waives such exemption. It shall not be a cause of challenge that a juror has read in the newspapers an account of the commission of the crime with which the prisoner is charged, if such juror shall state on oath that he believes he can render an impartial verdict according to the law and the evidence.

In the trial of any criminal cause, the fact that a person called as a juror has formed an opinion or impression, based upon rumor or upon newspaper statements (about the truth of which he has expressed no opinion,) shall not disqualify him to serve as a juror in such case, if he shall upon oath state that he believes he can fairly and impartially render a verdict therein, in accordance with the law and the evidence, and the court shall be satisfied of the truth of such statement.

705 ILCS 305/10.2

Excusing Prospective Jurors: Hardship

(a) The county boards of the respective counties, the jury commissioners for those counties which have been appointed under the Jury Commission Act, or a jury administrator shall submit questionnaires to prospective jurors to inquire as to their qualifications for jury service and as to the hardship that jury service would pose to the prospective jurors. Upon prior approval by the chief judge of the judicial circuits in which a county board, jury administrator, or jury commissioners are situated, the county board, jury administrator, or jury commissioners shall excuse a prospective juror from jury service if the prospective juror shows that such service would impose an undue hardship on account of the nature of the prospective juror's occupation, business affairs, physical health, family situation, active duty in the Illinois National Guard or Illinois Naval Militia, or other personal affairs, and cause his or her name to be returned to the jury list or general jury list.

(b) When an undue hardship caused by a family situation is due to the prospective juror being the primary care giver of a person with a mental or physical disability, a person with a medically diagnosed behavior problem, or a child under age 12, then the county board, jury commissioners or jury administrator shall excuse such a prospective juror, if it finds that no reasonable alternative care is feasible which would not impose an undue hardship on the prospective juror or the person for whom the prospective juror is providing care, or both.

705 ILCS 305/10.3

Excusing Prospective Jurors: Nursing Mothers

Any mother nursing her child shall, upon request, be excused from jury service.

705 ILCS 305/10.4

Removal of Prospective Juror Due to Total and Permanent Disability

If a prospective juror is found to be unqualified due to the existence of a total and permanent disability or is excused for undue hardship that is due to the existence of a total and permanent disability, the county board, jury administrator, or jury commissioners shall permanently exclude the prospective juror from all current and subsequent jury lists or general jury lists. Proof of total and permanent disability shall be either:

(1) a written letter from a licensed physician that

states the prospective juror has a total and permanent disability as defined in this Section, describes the disability, explains how it prevents the prospective juror from serving as a juror, and states that the prospective juror will never be able to serve as a juror;

(2) a copy of an individualized education program

plan for the prospective juror who participates in a special education program or receives transition or supported employment services under Article 14 of the School Code, submitted by the prospective juror or his or her legal guardian; or

(3) a copy of a court order for guardianship showing that the juror has been adjudged totally without capacity and a plenary guardian has been appointed.

The county board, jury administrator, or jury commissioners shall create and maintain a list of persons to be permanently excluded from any jury list or general jury list pursuant to this Section. The county board, jury administrator, or jury commissioners shall notify a prospective juror, or his or her legal guardian, when the juror is permanently excluded from all current and subsequent jury lists or general jury lists due to total and permanent disability.

For the purposes of this Section, "total and permanent disability" means any physical or mental impairment, disease, or loss of a permanent nature that prevents performance of the duties of a juror. "Total and permanent disability" does not include an impairment or disease that is transitory or minor in nature or is capable of being improved.

705 ILCS 305/21

Jurors Passed Upon in Panels of Four

Upon the impaneling of any jury in any civil cause now pending, or to be hereafter commenced in any court in this state, it shall be the duty of the court, upon request of either party to the suit, or upon its own motion, to order its full number of jurors into the jury box, before either party shall be required to examine any of the jurors touching their qualifications to try any such causes: Provided, that the jury shall be passed upon and accepted in panels of four by the parties, commencing with the plaintiff. Alternate jurors shall be passed upon separately.

735 ILCS 5/2-1101

Challenges for Cause

735 ILCS 5/2-1106

Peremptory Challenges: Alternate Jurors

(a) Each side shall be entitled to 5 peremptory challenges. If there is more than one party on any side, the court may allow each side additional peremptory challenges, not to exceed 3, on account of each additional party on the side having the greatest number of parties. Each side shall be allowed an equal number of peremptory challenges. If the parties on a side are unable to agree upon the allocation of peremptory challenges among themselves, the allocation shall be determined by the court.

(b) The court may direct that 1 or 2 jurors in addition to the regular panel be impanelled to serve as alternate jurors. Alternate jurors, in the sequence in which they are ordered into the jury box, shall replace jurors who, prior to the time the jury retires to consider its verdict, become unable to perform their duties. Alternate jurors shall be drawn in the same manner, have the same qualifications, be subject to the same examination and challenges, take the same oath, and have the same functions, powers, facilities, and privileges as the principal jurors. An alternate juror who does not replace a principal juror shall be discharged at the time the jury retires to consider its verdict. If alternate jurors are called each side shall be allowed one additional peremptory challenge, regardless of the number of alternate jurors called. The additional peremptory challenge may be used only against an alternate juror, but any unexercised peremptory challenges may be used against an alternate juror.

(Source: P.A. 83-707.)

Supreme Court Rule 233

Parties' Order of Proceeding

The parties shall proceed at all stages of the trial, including the selection of prospective jurors as specified in Rule 234, opening and closing statements, the offering of evidence, and the examination of witnesses, in the order in which they appear in the pleadings unless otherwise agreed by all parties or ordered by the court. In consolidated cases, third-party proceedings, and all other cases not otherwise provided for, the court shall designate the order.

Amended effective July 1, 1975.

Committee Comments
(Revised July 1, 1975)

This is Rule 6.2 of the Uniform Rules for the Circuit Courts of Illinois.

The phrase "as specified in Rule 234" was added in 1975 to reflect changes in the procedure for conduct of the voir dire examination of prospective jurors, effected at the same time by amendments to Rule 234.

Supreme Court Rule 234

Voir Dire Examination of Jurors and Cautionary Instructions

The court shall conduct the voir dire examination of prospective jurors by putting to them questions it thinks appropriate touching upon their qualifications to serve as jurors in the case on trial. The court may permit the parties to submit additional questions to it for further inquiry if it thinks they are appropriate, and shall permit the parties to supplement the examination by such direct inquiry as the court deems proper for a reasonable period of time depending upon the length of examination by the court, the complexity of the case, and the nature and extent of the damages. Questions shall not directly or indirectly concern matters of law or instructions. The court shall acquaint prospective jurors with the general duties and responsibilities of jurors.

Amended effective July 1, 1975; amended August 9, 1983, effective October 1, 1983; amended April 3, 1997, effective May 1, 1997.

Committee Comments
(Revised July 1, 1975)

Rule 234 was amended in 1975 to emphasize the duty of the judge to manage the voir dire examination. Under the rule as amended the judge must put to the prospective jurors such questions as he thinks necessary and then may either permit the attorneys or the parties to supplement the examination by putting questions directly to the prospective jurors or may require them to submit the questions to him, in which event he will put such of the questions submitted as he thinks proper

Illinois Pattern Jury Instruction 1.01

Preliminary Cautionary Instructions

[1] Now that the evidence has concluded, I will instruct you as to the law and your duties.

[2] The law regarding this case is contained in the instructions I will give to you. You must consider the Court's instructions as a whole, not picking out some instructions and disregarding others.

[3] It is your duty to resolve this case by determining the facts based on the evidence and following the law given in the instructions. Your verdict must not be based upon speculation, prejudice, or sympathy. [Each party, whether a [(i.e., corporation, partnership, etc.)] or an individual, should receive your same fair consideration.] My rulings, remarks or instructions do not indicate any opinion as to the facts.

[4] You will decide what facts have been proven. Facts may be proven by evidence or reasonable inferences drawn from the evidence. Evidence consists of the testimony of witnesses and of exhibits admitted by the court. You should consider all the evidence without regard to which party produced it. You may use common sense gained from your experiences in life, in evaluating what you see and hear during trial.

[5] You are the only judges of the credibility of the witnesses. You will decide the weight to be given to the testimony of each of them. In evaluating the credibility of a witness, you may consider that witness' ability and opportunity to observe, memory, manner, interest, bias, qualifications, experience, and any previous inconsistent statement or act by the witness concerning an issue important to the case.

[6] You should not do any independent investigation or research on any subject relating to the case. What you may have seen or heard outside the courtroom is not evidence. This includes any press, radio, or television programs and it also includes any information available on the Internet. Such programs, reports, and information are not evidence and your verdict must not be influenced in any way by such material.

[7] For example, you must not use the Internet, [including Google,] [Wikipedia,] [[(insert current examples)]], or any other sources that you might use every day, to search for any information about the case, or the law which applies to the case, or the people involved in the case, including the parties, witnesses, lawyers, and judge.

[8] During the course of the trial, do not discuss this case with anyone--not even your own families or friends, and also not even among yourselves--until at the end of the trial when you have retired to the jury room to deliberate on your verdict. Even though this is hard to do, it will be a violation of these instructions and your oath if you discuss the case with anyone else.

[9] You must not provide any information about the case to anyone by any means at all, and this includes posting information about the case, or your thoughts about it, on any device or Internet site, including [blogs,] [chat-rooms,] or [[(insert current examples)]], or any social networking websites, such as [Twitter], [Facebook] or [[(insert current examples)]], or any other means.

[10] You cannot use any electronic devices or services to communicate about this case, Section 1, Page 3 of 17 and this includes [cell-phones,] [smart-phones,] [lap-tops,] [the Internet,] [[(insert current examples)]] and any other tools of technology. The use of any such devices or services in connection with your duties is prohibited.

[11] The reason for these instructions is that your verdict must be based only on the evidence presented in this courtroom and the law I [will provide] [have provided] to you in my instructions. It would be unfair to the parties and a violation of your oath to base your decision on information from outside this courtroom. You should feel free to remind each other that your verdict is to be based only on the evidence admitted in court and that you cannot use information from any other sources. If you become aware of any violation of these instructions, it is your legal duty to report this to me immediately.

[12] Disobeying these instructions could cause a mistrial, meaning all of our efforts have been wasted and we would have to start over again with a new trial. If you violate these instructions you could be found in contempt of court.

[13] Pay close attention to the testimony as it is given. At the end of the trial you must make your decision based on what you recall of the evidence. You will not receive a written transcript of the testimony when you retire to the jury room.

[14] An opening statement is what an attorney expects the evidence will be. A closing argument is given at the conclusion of the case and is a summary of what an attorney contends the evidence has shown. If any statement or argument of an attorney is not supported by the law or the evidence, you should disregard that statement or argument.

[15] During this trial, you may be permitted to ask questions of [certain] witnesses, but you must follow the procedures that I describe: If you have a question for a witness and you believe the answer would be helpful to you in understanding the case, then after the lawyers have completed their questions, but before that witness is excused, I will give you a chance to submit your question in writing. I will have you write your question on a piece of paper and hand it to the bailiff. [The court may now describe specific procedures to be used. See Comment for examples.] You should not write your name or juror

number with the question. Also, you should not discuss your questions with your fellow jurors at this time. You may submit one or more questions or no question at all. It is up to you. Please keep in mind, though, that you should only ask a question if you think it is important to your ability to decide the issues in this case fairly. You should be sure you are asking a question and not making a comment. You should not use your questions to argue with a witness or to express opinions about a witness's testimony. Your role is to be an impartial fact-finder. The purpose of your question should be to clarify testimony that you have not understood or that has failed to address a factual question that you believe is important. After the bailiff has collected the pieces of paper and given them to me, I will decide whether the law allows the question to be asked of the witness. Not all questions can be asked or asked using the wording that was submitted. The rules of evidence might not permit me to ask your question. You shall not concern yourself with the reason for the exclusion or modification Section 1, Page 4 of 17 of any question submitted. If I cannot ask your question or if I rephrase it, please do not be offended and do not let it affect your judgment of the evidence or the witness in any way. If the question is allowed, I will ask the question of the witness and the attorneys may then ask some follow-up questions. Please do not speak directly to me, the lawyers, or the witnesses.

Instruction, Notes on Use and Comment revised January 2011; [15]Instruction and Notes on Use on 1.01 [15] approved June 1, 2012;[15]Comment approved June 21, 2012.

Notes on Use.

Some trial judges give cautionary instructions at the beginning of the trial; some give them at the close of the trial before the deliberations; and some give them throughout the trial. Although the trial judge has discretion as to when to give cautionary instructions, the committee suggests that cautionary instructions

1.01 [3]-[14][15] should be given at the beginning of the trial, 1.01 [1]-[14] should be given at the end of trial, and that the instructions reminding jurors to refrain from doing outside research [1.01 [6] and [7]), from discussing the case with anyone (1.01 [8] and [9]), and from using electronic devices in connection with their duties as jurors (1.01 [10]) should be repeated throughout the trial.

For any of the cautionary instructions that refer to particular forms of technology, such as 1.01 [7], [9] and [10], judges should feel free to add new examples as they become available.

The numbers in the brackets preceding each paragraph refer to the Comments

and Notes on Use following the instruction and should not be included when the instruction is given.

The instruction, with brackets removed, should be given as a single instruction.

As to 1.01 [15], on April 3, 2012, the Illinois Supreme Court adopted Rule 243, which explicitly authorizes judges to allow jurors to submit written questions to certain or all witnesses in civil jury trials in Illinois. The rule outlines the procedures to be followed, see Supreme Court Rule 243, but makes clear that the trial judge has discretion whether to permit questions. See Committee Comments to Supreme Court Rule 243.

Although Rule 243 identifies certain procedures for the submission of juror questions to witnesses, it also indicates that trial judges are free to work out the details of the procedures on their own. See id. The Comment provides approaches that other judges have tried to ensure that jurors feel comfortable asking questions.

Rule 243 also makes clear that the judge will review the questions outside of the presence of the jury, read each question for the record, and hear objections, if any, from the lawyers. The judge will rule on whether the question can be asked, including any rephrasing of the question. If the question can be asked, then the judge will ask it and instruct the witness to answer only the question asked. The lawyers will have a chance to ask follow-up questions of the witness limited to the scope of the new testimony.

NOTES

NOTES

NOTES

NOTES

NOTES

NOTES

NOTES

NOTES

NOTES

NOTES

NOTES

www.ingramcontent.com/pod-product-compliance
Lightning Source LLC
La Vergne TN
LVHW082345200926
848481LV00012B/3459
* 9 7 8 1 5 9 9 3 2 8 1 2 6 *